If Dr. Luke bent over backward to emphasize one thing, it was that the disciples weren't up to the task in front of them until they were empowered. Larry Walkemeyer provides a road map for those seeking empowerment for multiplication, and there's nobody I'd rather listen to on this subject. Larry Walkemeyer lives and breathes multiplication and models the empowerment of the Holy Spirit in his own life.

Peyton Jones
CEO, NewBreed Training
Author of *Church Plantology*

In *The Empowerment Factor*, Larry gets right at the heart of both the symptom and solution to our disciple-making challenge in the West. From his personal experience, he gives us insights into empowering prayer as well as the perspective, posture, and practices we need to see a movement of God. This is how to dream big!

Bill Couchenour
Director of Deployment, Exponential

If you are curious about how to live empowered by the Holy Spirit and empower others to accomplish Jesus' mission in the world, *The Empowerment Factor* is your go-to resource.
This book provides a biblically rooted and evaluative process to help you develop a greater capacity to empower others within your circle of influence. We all want to experience a 21st-century revival movement, but it's important to know that every revival movement throughout history began with one prayerful soul fired up for the Acts 1:8 mission of the church. That one person might be you or the person you pass this book onto! Don't just read this book—read it and pass it on to someone else!

Dr. Ed Love
Executive Director of Church Multiplication and Discipleship,
The Wesleyan Church

If every pastor, seminary professor, denominational leader, and business leader reads and employees the principles in this book ... we will experience renewal/revival on an unprecedented mass level.

Jason Garcia
Co-Founder/Director, Leadership Architects
Founder/Director, Rize Network

This is a must-read for all leaders who are longing for the empowering presence of the Holy Spirit to facilitate transformational multiplication that begins in us and then [moves] through us for others as we live empowered lives that empower others to do the same. Dr. Walkemeyer's breakdown of one's Personal Multiplication Capacity (PMC) is incredibly helpful and challenging. The practical wisdom that this book contains arises from a lived reality of a man who sits daily in the presence of the One who empowers. May we all do the same!

Mike Chong Perkinson
Director of Multiplication, Free Methodist Southern California
Co-Founder and Senior Developer, The Praxis Center for Church Development
President and Dean of Church & Ministry, Trivium Institute of Leader Development

Every church planter, pastor, and leader should read this book! Having personally experienced the impact of Larry's empowering leadership, I can attest that he provides a field-tested blueprint for unleashing the Kingdom potential within individuals and teams. What I love about this book is that it shifts the discussion away from ministry strategies and puts it squarely on the power of personal and intentional disciple-making relationships. At every level, this biblical priority is what the church desperately needs. My life has been changed by the principles in this book, and I am certain yours will be too.

Rev. Dr. JR Rushik
Executive Director, Church Development Network

God has discipled Larry Walkemeyer to disciple others. So many today experience subtraction or merely addition in their ministries. But God has raised up Larry to share his lifelong Kingdom multiplication model. Are you a leader? Pastor Larry helps us understand that the answer is a thousand times yes (Matthew 20:16-20)! Embrace the concepts found in this book and begin to develop others. Learn to use these tools to more effectively disciple others. I am excited to grow my Personal Multiplication Capacity (PMC) and use The Empowerment Factor to empower our church leadership. The most impactful leaders are often the least known leaders!

Rev. Dr. John Teter
Holy Faith Fellowship, Compton
Director, Antioch Church Planting Network
Author, *The Power of the 72*

Reading *The Empowerment Factor* was like walking through the last 16 years of being personally discipled, led, and developed by Dr. Larry Walkemeyer. To see this process and these principles laid out in a format that any leader can pick up and immediately begin to live out gives me hope for a discipleship-empowering and Spirit-fueled multiplication movement that leaves a lasting impact. My life has been forever changed by what you will read, and I know yours will be too!

Rev. Sean Fenner
Co-Lead Pastor, Light & Life Christian Fellowship
City to City Los Angeles Catalyst

Ten years ago I walked into Pastor Larry's church and encountered a Spirit-empowered church that believed in empowering others! A novice in campus ministry, Pastor Larry took me under his leadership so that over the next 10 years I experienced the vision, principles, and strategies outlined in this book. The things Pastor Larry writes about are not only what he has practiced for decades, but what continues to bear tangible fruit in his life. If you desire to be a faithful and fruitful leader, read and implement *The Empowerment Factor*!

Rev. Joel Silva
Co-Lead Pastor, Light & Life Christian Fellowship

An important and beautiful book. *The Empowerment Factor* is crafted with meaning and intimacy. It is impossible not to be spiritually changed once it's been read. I have been personally discipled by Larry, and these principles have empowered my life. For those who want to live with purpose and develop the strength to empower others, this is a must-read. It will inspire you and reignite your passion to serve. Empowerment is for all of us who want to flourish in our faith and reach others to fulfill their potential as God intended. If you want to revolutionize your Christian walk, read *The Empowerment Factor*.

Vinicio J. López, Ed.D.
Vice President, Skyline College
Board of Administrators, Light & Life Church

Larry Walkemeyer has written a powerful must-read for anyone wanting to become empowered to create and nurture disciples who will then create more disciples. It is a transformative guide for those seeking to unlock their Personal Multiplication Capacity (PMC). This book is not just a read; it's a guide to embracing a Spirit-empowered life, navigating challenges, and becoming a catalyst for positive change in the lives of others. Larry has discipled me using these principles, and I have discovered an adventurous, abundant, and fruitful life available to empower others. It's life-changing!

Greg Gaskill
Owner/Managing Partner, Summerlon Corporation

Larry Walkemeyer's *The Empowerment Factor* is a much-needed, thorough, masterful, and practical walk-through on how we can shift from addition to multiplication in Christian ministry. Larry provides a clear Personal Multiplication Capacity tool and then proceeds to show us how to increase our influence. This book will help us move from, as Larry puts it, "the 'smoke' of the Christian religion to the 'fire' of the Spirit's presence." Walkemeyer opened my eyes to see the relationship between expectation and faith, breathing and prayer, humility and confidence, rivers and lakes, exclusivity and discipling, as well as failure and failure to launch. I highly recommend this book from Larry, who is not just a great thinker but a strategic empowerer!

JD Pearring
Director, Excel Leadership Network

We've been given not only a mission by Christ but also the power and model for fulfilling this mission. *The Empowerment Factor* provides us with a helpful paradigm to maximize our missional potential by recognizing the synergistic relationship of our Spirit-empowered life and our empowerment of others in God's mission. I commend this book to any Christian leader who longs for greater effectiveness in fulfilling Jesus' continued mission on earth.

Dustin Weber
Executive Director, Mission Igniter

LARRY WALKEMEYER

The Empowerment Factor

Increasing Your Personal Multiplication Capacity

FOREWORD
RALPH MOORE

EXPONENTIAL

Exponential is a growing movement of activists committed to the multiplication of healthy new churches. Exponential Resources spotlights actionable principles, ideas, and solutions for the accelerated multiplication of healthy, reproducing faith communities. For more information, visit exponential.org.

The Empowerment Factor: Increasing Your Personal Multiplication Capacity

Copyright © 2024 by Larry Walkemeyer

All rights reserved. No part of this book, including icons and images, may be reproduced in any manner without prior written permission from copyright holder, except where noted in the text and in the case of brief quotations embodied in critical articles and reviews.

Unless otherwise indicated, all Scripture quotations are taken from the Holy Bible, New International Version®, NIV®. Copyright © 1973, 1978, 1984, 2011 by Biblica, Inc.® Used by permission of Zondervan. All rights reserved worldwide. www.zondervan.com. The "NIV" and "New International Version" are trademarks registered in the United States Patent and Trademark Office by Biblica, Inc.®

Scriptures marked ESV are taken from The Holy Bible, English Standard Version® (ESV®) Copyright © 2001 by Crossway, a publishing ministry of Good News Publishers. All rights reserved.

Scripture quotations marked ISV have been taken from the Holy Bible: International Standard Version® Release 2.0. Copyright © 1996-2013 by the ISV Foundation. Used by permission of Davidson Press, LLC.

Scripture quotations marked TLB are taken from The Living Bible, copyright © 1971 by Tyndale House Foundation. Used by permission of Tyndale House Publishers, Carol Stream, Illinois 60188. All rights reserved.

Scripture quotations taken from the (LSB®) Legacy Standard Bible®, Copyright © 2021 by The Lockman Foundation. Used by permission. All rights reserved. Managed in partnership with Three Sixteen Publishing Inc. LSBible.org and 316publishing.com.

Any italics in Scripture quotations have been added by the author.

ISBN: 978-1-62424-122-2 (paperback)

ISBN: 978-1-62424-123-9 (ebook/epub)

Editor: Karen Cain

Cover: Sabir Robinson

Interior design: ArtSpeak Creative

Contents

Foreword ix

Introduction: The Invitation to Empowerment 13

Chapter 1: Your Personal Multiplication Capacity Revealed. 17

PART 1: EMPOWERED

Chapter 2: The Empowered Priesthood—Yes, That's You!. 33

Chapter 3: Empowered Leadership—Are You a Leader or Follower? 41

Chapter 4: The Position of Empowerment—Suntans and Rivers 49

Chapter 5: The Seat of Empowerment—The Best Seat in the House 55

Chapter 6: The Expectation of Empowerment—Faithing Your Future 61

Chapter 7: The Air of Empowerment—Breathing Well 65

Chapter 8: The Words of Empowerment—Power Bread 73

Chapter 9: The Habits of Empowerment—The Dance of Discipline 79

Chapter 10: The Crew of Empowerment—The Johari Team 87

PART 2: EMPOWERING

Chapter 11: Empowering—The Jesus Ministry Method 95

Chapter 12: Empowering Your Circles of Influence—Playing Favorites 107

Chapter 13: The Empowering Connection—The Question of Love. 115

Chapter 14: The Empowering Cause—The Question of Mission 121

Chapter 15: The Empowering Key—The Question of Trust. 127

Chapter 16: Empowering Training—The Question of Equipping 135

Chapter 17: Empowering Opportunities—The Question of Open Doors 143

Chapter 18: Empowering Relationships—The Question of Team 149

Chapter 19: The Empowering Pay-off—The Question of Reward 153

Chapter 20: The Final Product—Your Highest Kingdom Impact 159

Additional Resources 163

Foreword

I'm convicted—Larry Walkemeyer got to me through this book! Like many others, I spend my days conspiring to equip others for ministry. However, my empowering them to serve without empowerment from the Spirit is a losing game. *The Empowerment Factor* sheds light on the connection between being empowered and empowering others, as emphasized in Scripture.

When Jesus appeared to his followers after his resurrection, he imparted authority, responsibility, and spiritual power to them. We're familiar with authority and responsibility in the Great Commission (Matthew 28:16-20). In the Gospel of John, Jesus references his source of power linked to the miraculous: "Peace be with you! As the Father has sent me, I am sending you" (John 20:21). The disciples were not merely bystanders but rather commissioned agents carrying on Jesus' work—thanks to his empowerment.

Later, Jesus breathed on his disciples and said, "Receive the Holy Spirit" (John 20:22). He empowered them spiritually, enabling them to execute their calling. They would empower others with freedom to act and power to support their actions.

Jesus gives the Church leadership gifts (Spirit-empowered people) to equip others for ministry. But if we fail our people regarding their Holy Spirit empowerment, we're dooming them to frustration.

In his letter to the Ephesians, the apostle Paul highlights the importance of leadership gifts in empowering others for ministry. He writes, "So Christ himself gave the apostles, the prophets, the evangelists, the pastors and teachers, to equip his people for works of service, so that the body of Christ may be built up" (Ephesians 4:11-12).

This statement underscores the importance of embracing the fullness of our calling and relying on the Holy Spirit's empowerment to fulfill it.

The Holy Spirit gives these leadership abilities so that we may equip and empower others rather than use our abilities for personal recognition or authority. Walkemeyer emphasizes that if our disciples fail to recognize and cultivate their empowerment by the Holy Spirit, they will struggle to fulfill their calling. They will experience frustration in their ministry efforts.

Larry says that we too often settle for the "smoke" of Christianity instead of the "fire" of the Spirit's presence. We rely on the truth of the Bible for our doctrine and polity but not on the power of the Spirit to drive our calling. We seek excuses and escape clauses rather than seeking the Spirit's assistance to do what we can't do on our own.

He describes how we dumb down our calling in vain efforts to fit our responsibilities into our human comfort zone. Dumbing down scrapes the corners off of God's purposes for our lives. This book anticipates the results of our reductions with Henry Blackaby's words: "The Holy Spirit doesn't need to equip you for what you're not going to do."[1]

---

[1] Henry and Melvin Blackaby, "Experiencing the Spirit", 2009, p. 62

We are empowered so that we may help others find empowerment.

Reliance on religious rituals without the empowerment of the Spirit limits the effectiveness and impact of ministry. Larry challenges readers to seek the assistance of the Holy Spirit in accomplishing what they cannot achieve on their own. Instead of seeking excuses or comfort zones, believers are encouraged to embrace the power and guidance of the Holy Spirit to fulfill their God-given purpose.

The Empowerment Factor by Larry Walkemeyer is a powerful reminder of the indispensable role of the Holy Spirit's empowerment in ministry. The book challenges believers to move beyond the mere trappings of religious rituals and embrace the dynamic power of the Spirit. By recognizing and cultivating their empowerment, believers can effectively equip and empower others for ministry, fulfilling their God-given calling with greater effectiveness and impact. We must strive to be empowered while empowering others. Through the Holy Spirit's empowerment, lives transform, and God's Kingdom advances.

Having read the book twice, I'm now revising a manuscript I hope to work into a book on disciple-making. Larry Walkemeyer has me revisiting and reviewing a lifetime of efforts to equip others. I'm looking for places where I may have shortchanged others regarding the power available to them.

Ralph Moore
Founder, Hope Chapel Movement
Church Multiplication Catalyst, Exponential

How do you evaluate your PMC? How do you grow your PMC?

Are you willing to go on a personal exploration of how impactful your life can be?

The following pages will share the call to a more empowered life, the means to live more fully empowered, and the impact of that outflow of power to effectively empower others.

John Wesley's last words are some of my favorites. I could die with these words on my lips. They are words to die by, but more importantly, they are words to live by: *"The best of all, God is with us."* His indwelling Spirit is our daily empowerment to a life of multiplicative impact.

CHAPTER 1
Your Personal Multiplication Capacity Revealed

Harold Taves is still ministering with greater impact than ever ... even though he departed for Home a few decades ago. If you Google "Reverend Harold Taves," you come up empty-handed. Yet, Pastor Taves lived with the Empowerment Factor and a high PMC.

Pastor Taves pastored small Holiness churches like the one I attended in rural Kansas. He never led a church of more than 80 people. He never wrote a book or was quoted in a magazine. His sermons were homiletically weak. What Harold *was* known for, however, were godliness, prayerfulness, humility, and faith. His life was filled with the presence and power of the Holy Spirit.

Harold was not pursuing notoriety or the fastest-growing church. He believed in the multiplication of disciples and the empowering of those around him. His passion was to raise up believers who would leverage their faith and gifts to influence others. Consequently, he poured his life into individuals like me.

The result of Harold's ministry was that over a dozen members of that obscure church went into full-time ministry, and thousands of lives have been changed because of it. Dozens of other disciples went on to impact their workplace, their relatives, and their social circles, reaching hundreds more with the life and love of Christ.

Recently when I was at one of our daughter churches and praying for a ministry couple being sent out to plant a "granddaughter" church, I thought of Pastor Taves. His PMC was still creating ripple effects 55 years later, despite the fact that he never lived to hear the term.

We will never know the Kingdom impact of the unknown "Harolds" who were empowered by the Spirit and lived to empower others. What we *can* know is how to live an empowered life and how to empower others. We can grow our PMC.

What Is Personal Multiplication Capacity?

Personal Multiplication Capacity (PMC) is a way of thinking about your life and your leadership. It is an approach that increases the enjoyment and impact of your spiritual life. It's a way to do ministry like Jesus did. It is a paradigm, not a personality inventory. It reveals and invites. It is a shaping tool that you ask the Spirit to apply to your life daily. If you choose to let it, PMC can transform your mindset and consequently revolutionize your life and impact.

PMC demands that you ask yourself two vital questions daily, and even throughout your day: 1) How can I live Spirit-empowered today? and 2) Who can I help empower today?

The Personal Multiplication Capacity tool is subjective because it is self-evaluative. Consequently, you can't really compare your score with someone else's. Your self-analysis is filtered through your unique personality. For example, positivity is one of my top strengths.

Therefore, I tend to be a little unrealistic, as in "the glass is half full" even if it has just a few drops of water in it! I probably tend to score myself a bit higher than is objectively true.

But the more objective you can be, the more this tool will help you. And as you use it, you will find ways to invite the observations of others into your life to help you be more honest and think more clearly about your PMC rating.

This PMC rating is not at all like an Enneagram number, which is static. Quite the opposite. This PMC score is a constantly shifting designation simply meant to help you grow "up and to the right" in your Personal Multiplication Capacity. Your score changes even during the course of a day.

The idea is not to try to slavishly keep track of your PMC score, but to be "transformed by the renewing of your mind" (Romans 12:2). This is a "between you and God" dialogue informed by a certain paradigm of living and ministry.

Pastor Harold Taves never had an inventory like this, but he carried a PMC tool around in his heart and head. He wasn't fixated on how to grow his church but on how to accomplish Christ's Acts 1:8 mission. He got up every day asking, "HOW can I live Spirit-empowered today?" And "WHO can I help empower today?" That's the essence of the PMC tool.

Charted assessment tools, whether recorded in writing or carried as a mental picture, can aid us in growing our ministry effectiveness in the right direction.

The Personal Multiplication Capacity tool is a simple graph in which the coordinates are multiplied to create a personal assessment score that reflects your current and potential effectiveness at multiplying ministry.

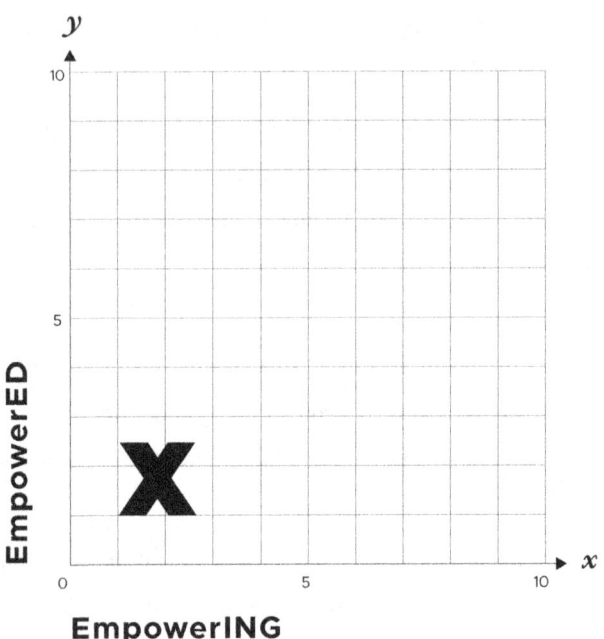

The *y* line runs vertically and is demarcated 1 to 10. The *x* line runs horizontally and is also demarcated from 1 to 10.

The *y* line is titled "EMPOWERED" and represents our current level of Spirit-fullness.

Since the *y* line stretches vertically, it illustrates the RECEIVING of power from on high.

It is the first half of Acts 1:8 (ESV): "You will receive power when the Holy Spirit has come upon you." This is an ongoing relational dynamic with the Holy Spirit.

The *x* line is titled "EMPOWERING" and represents our current level of empowering those in our circle of relationships.

Since the *x* line reaches horizontally, it illustrates the RELEASING of spiritual power to others. It is the second half of Acts 1:8: "And you will be my witnesses." It is a channeling of *our* spiritual empowerment into the transmission of our faith, wisdom, ministry, and spiritual life into *others* and then commissioning those others to go to others. This is an ongoing relational dynamic with the people in our circles of influence.

The purpose and potential of the PMC tool is to invite every believer (and especially every leader) to grow into and live with both a high *y* and *x* number, producing a high PMC.

J.R. Rushik has been the catalyst for 300 churches being started in the last two years. As I have observed his dynamic ministry, there are two keys to his effectiveness. First, pray and pray some more, depending on the work of the Spirit. Second, encourage ordinary people to hear God's calling to extraordinary mission, including church planting. Then, empower them to do it! J.R. has a high PMC.

Our level of EMPOWERED Spirit-fullness (our *y* score) is not a static number. The Spirit does not diminish, but our own yieldedness and attunement to the Spirit do, and consequently, "fullness" changes. This creates the fluctuation in our *y* number.

Likewise, our *x* value of EMPOWERING others also varies during days, years, and seasons of our lives. Some of this fluctuation is due to our discipleship commitment, our leadership models, or our church addition vs. church multiplication thinking. Other causes of inconsistency have to do with our own willingness to live selfless, servant-leader kinds of lives.

Our empowered (*y*) and our empowering (*x*) levels are connected and interactive with one another. They are like a baby's mobile hanging with just two toy animals over a crib. The baby can't touch one animal without impacting the other. But the animal the baby touches will swing a lot more than the other.

Unlike a baby's mobile, however, there is a definitive order to x and y, even as there is an order to Acts 1:8. Unlike the alphabet, y (empowered) always precedes x (empowering) in this process. We receive power so that we might release power to others.

What does the letter "Y" of the vertical axis look like to you? To me, it looks like an individual with both arms extended in praise to the Lord. Or it looks like a child saying to their father, "Pick me up, Daddy." Or it looks like someone receiving a gift from above. This is the interface between the Spirit and you that leads to living empowered.

What does the letter "X" say to you? For me the letter "X" of the horizontal axis brings to mind three distinct images:

> The x reminds me of the cross and Jesus saying that we must take up our cross and lay down our lives for others daily.
>
> Note the two lines intersecting to form the x. We are empowered in order to intersect with the lives of others and become an empowering force.
>
> The message of the x to me is multiplication. This intersection of an empowered life with the life of another believer is how empowering multiplication occurs.

Empowered x Empowering = Personal Multiplication Capacity

When the y value (empowered) is multiplied by our x value (empowering), our theoretical Personal Multiplication Capacity is created. Our PMC is created by how "Spirit-full" we are living as we invest in empowering those around us.

For example, a believer living at a 7 value on the empowered y axis who is following a model of doing ministry mostly solo (perhaps a 3 on the x axis) will have a PMC of 21.

Or a pastor who is really effective at leadership development (perhaps a 7 on the x axis) but who is operating mostly on personal charisma and self-reliance (perhaps a 2 on the y axis) will have a PMC of 14.

Another example might be a disciple who is really growing in their faith, gaining in their knowledge of the Word, developing a habit of prayer, and giving up bad lifestyle choices (perhaps a 6 on the y axis) but who has no vision or traction to transmit their life of faith to others (a 1 on the x axis) has a PMC of 6.

A large-church pastor who is spiritually gifted and an excellent teacher but who is only trying to grow the church instead of making disciples who make disciples might be a 6 on the y axis but only a 3 on the x scale, and thus would have a PMC of 18.

The beauty and power of PMC is that it has nothing to do with church size and everything to do with Kingdom impact. It refuses to take the short-term view of "addition only" growth and instead looks at the enduring and expanding impact of empowering others into multiplication. It is not talent-based but based on Spiritual abiding connected to Spiritual-investing. It prioritizes Kingdom growth over decades, not years.

So there could be a Harold Taves who is perhaps an 8 on the empowered scale and an 8 on the empowering scale, and his PMC is 64. The rippling and multiplication impact of his ministry will reach far past the size of his church and the length of his life.

It is rare in my experience to find someone who I think has a score of 80 or higher. Living daily in the fullness of the Spirit at 9 or 10 while empowering others at a level of 8+ is uncommon for a leader in God's Kingdom. Perhaps the clearest historical example of this type of uncommon leader outside of Scripture is John Wesley.

John Wesley's quest was for a moment-by-moment surrender to the Spirit's will and a reliance upon his power. Wesley wrote regarding sanctification in his journal, "I believe it to be an inward thing, namely, the life of God in the soul of man; a participation of the Divine nature; the mind of Christ; or the renewal of our heart after the image of Him that created us" (*Journal*, Sept. 1793).[5]

This pursuit of the empowered life was matched only in Wesley's intensity to empower others. As Winfield Bevins points out in his book *Marks of a Movement*, "Wesley personally worked to empower thousands of laity, many who later became leaders of the movement. These ordinary, non-ordained Christian men and women became the foundation of the next generation as the movement spread across the Western world in the eighteenth and nineteenth centuries."[6]

EMPOWERED describes living in a posture to RECEIVE maximum spiritual power. It is:

Spirit-fullness

Spirit-dependence

A life being daily shaped by the disciplines of the Spirit

Abiding in the Vine

Contagious spiritual passion

Vibrant faith and confidence in God's power

A whole-hearted surrender to God's purposes

---

5   https://www.craigladams.com/Books/Wesley/page6/ Accessed October 4, 2023.

6   https://www.seedbed.com/six-marks-of-the-wesleyan-movement/

A holiness of lifestyle with a sensitivity not to grieve the Spirit

A spiritual ear trained toward the Father's voice and the Spirit's nudges

An understanding and embracing of natural God-given strengths and talents

A recognition, appreciation, and application of personal spiritual gifts

An increasing demonstration of the fruit of the Spirit

Characteristics and leadership qualities that people admire and follow due to an integrity of life

A clear vision about one's mission in life

***EMPOWERING* means living to IMPART maximum spiritual power to others. It is:**

Laying down your life to lift up the lives of others

Desiring to serve rather than to be served

In every situation asking, *How can I bless and lift this person?*

Identifying key individuals God is calling you to disciple

Making disciples who will make disciples

Inspiring others, breathing life and spirit into others

Encouraging others, instilling courage in others to be more, dream more, risk more

Training and releasing others in ways that often do not result in credit to the leader

Being vulnerable, sharing life and not just lessons

Trusting and delegating beyond normal comfort levels

- Risk-taking in ways that have the potential of making the leader look bad
- Doing life with a few who will catch the fire of the leader's life
- Launching disciples forward at sacrifice to yourself
- Turning the spotlight away from yourself and onto others
- Expecting those you are investing in to repeat the process with others

Take a moment with what you've read thus far and prayerfully answer the following question:

What do you think your current PMC score is?

Take a good look at how "Spirit-full," how passionate, how alive, how deep, how attuned to God's Word and Spirit you really are, and assign yourself a score between 1 and 10. Again, the numerical values are defined subjectively by you, with 1 being spiritually dull, dry, distracted, distant, disempowered and 10 being the most spiritually alive, surrendered, zealous, full of faith, you've ever been. This is your y (empowered) value.

Next, take a thorough, honest look at the individuals you are empowering to become disciple-makers and everyday missionaries. Analyze this relationally not corporately, individually not collectively—meaning don't give yourself a high score based on preaching to the congregation. This is communicating on a personal level to individuals and small groups in a way that is empowering them to "go." Assign yourself a rating between 1 and 10. A 1 means you are doing ministry alone with hardly a thought of how you can empower and launch others into their ministries. A 10 means you are highly prioritizing and effectively empowering people into their callings in a way that is being multiplied. This is your *x* (empowering) value.

Back to my personal story of ministry. I arrived at my first pastorate with my mind filled with addition not multiplication. I absolutely wanted to be empowered to reach the lost. But, honestly, I wasn't thinking much at all about empowering others. My mindset was "preach and gather," "preach and gather more," and "preach and gather more and more." And "gather" meant to gather around *me*, to listen to *me*, to build *my* vision, and to bring more people to listen to *me*.

Books on church growth, leadership, speaking, management, and success were my steady reading diet. I went to conferences led by those who had "made it" and had big churches to show for their efforts. My biggest question was how to be "successful" in ministry. I learned some really helpful principles. I would rush back from conferences to apply what had worked in a growing, suburban, monoethnic context to my declining, urban, multi-ethnic, gang-filled area of Long Beach.

An "addition-only" mindset had me trapped in a rush to personal success with the scoreboard being a tally of how many people showed up on Sunday. I didn't have time to slow down, go deep, and empower people to multiply disciples. My empowerment was focused on me.

My *y* number of empowered was pretty good, maybe a 6 or 7. But my *x* number of empowering others was maybe a 2 or 3. My PMC was between 12 and 21.

The PMC in Scripture:

It is instructive to see how often you find EMPOWERED and EMPOWERING together in Scripture. Consider just three examples. (The parentheses are added in the verses in an effort to capture how I view this intersection between empowered and empowering.)

John 20:21-22: "Again Jesus said, 'Peace be with you. As the Father has sent me, I am sending you' (EMPOWERING). And with that he breathed on them and said, 'Receive the Holy Spirit'" (EMPOWERED).

Jesus commissions his disciples with a powerful declaration of the scope and strategy of the ministry they are to embark on. It was a high call involving great trust to be sent in the same manner Jesus had been sent by the Father. They had watched and practiced his ministry, and now it was being fully entrusted to them.

But before they launched forth, Jesus had an essential gift for them. They needed his breath, his Spirit, to enter and infuse them with power. This same breath can be passed on *to* you and *through* you to others.

A few weeks later Jesus would issue these famous words:

Matthew 28:18-20: "Then Jesus came to them and said, 'All authority (EMPOWERED) in heaven and on earth has been given to me. Therefore go (EMPOWERING) and make disciples of all nations (EMPOWERING), baptizing them in the name of the Father and of the Son and of the Holy Spirit (EMPOWERED), and teaching them to obey everything I have commanded you (EMPOWERING). And surely I am with you always, (EMPOWERED) to the very end of the age.'"

Jesus' universal authority was being declared in one final statement, and a portion of that authority was being delegated to his disciples. They could use his name, his authority, his power. They were EMPOWERED. But this power was for a purpose. It was so they could go, baptize, teach, and command. Jesus was EMPOWERING them and entrusting them with his mission. Best of all, Jesus (via his Spirit) would be with them to continue to empower them for all the days of ministry ahead.

The apostle Paul echoes and expands on Jesus' approach to ministry:

Ephesians 4:11-12: "So Christ himself gave the apostles, the prophets, the evangelists, the pastors and teachers (EMPOWERED), to equip his people for works of service, so that the body of Christ may be built up" (EMPOWERING).

The roles and offices of the saints are a received gift from Christ himself. These assignments are a divine empowerment from which the disciples are to operate. What are they to do with these gifts? Empower others. They are to use their roles to multiply the ministry. Each of these five gifts is an equipping gift to be used to move the entire body into effective ministry.

Every Christ follower has a Personal Multiplication Capacity that is determined by how empowered they are by the Spirit and how empowering they are of others. Every believer can increase their PMC for a life of greater impact for the Kingdom.

In the following chapters, we will examine how to live a more EMPOWERED life and how to lead in a more EMPOWERING manner.

PART 1
EMPOWERED

CHAPTER 2

The Empowered Priesthood—
Yes, That's You!

Our Personal Multiplication Capacity (PMC) is directly tied to how we view ourselves and other believers. If we do not understand our calling and anointing as priests, and if we do not see the same potential in all other believers, our PMC will remain low. We will live dull and low-impact Christian lives. But there is another way ... an adventurous, abundant, fruitful life available.

Imagine you are one of Jesus' disciples in that upper room in Jerusalem as the Feast of Pentecost draws near. There is an electric anticipation in the atmosphere. After showing up for 40 days in all kinds of places after his crucifixion, Jesus has ascended to Heaven. Before he went, Jesus promised: "I am going to send you what my Father has promised; but stay in the city until you have been clothed with power from on high" (Luke 24:49). His last words echoed the promise: "You will receive power when the Holy Spirit has come upon you" (Acts 1:8, ESV).

It's been 10 days since Jesus made that final statement. You and about 120 others have been meeting almost non-stop. You have been praying to the Father in Jesus' name that he will indeed send this new power and that you would be blessed enough to receive it. You wonder whether only the apostles will receive it, or whether it will come to all of Jesus' faithful followers like yourself. You try to imagine what that new power will be like. What will it enable you to be and do?

Abruptly, the strange sound of a strong wind fills the room, but there isn't even a breeze blowing. Everyone is standing in stunned silence, listening in awe, wondering what's next. Suddenly, something like a bonfire appears near the ceiling in the middle of the room. As you watch in wonderment, the bonfire begins to break apart, sending small flames throughout the room. The flames stop directly over each person's head. Your friends Joseph, Benjamin, and Salome each have a small fire over their heads. You reach up over your head to see whether you feel anything, but there is nothing. Yet Salome is pointing to you, exclaiming, "You've got one too!"

Immediately you feel an inner surge of inner strength. It is beyond emotion. It is not physical, yet it is the most real and wonderful thing you have ever experienced. You just have to burst out in glory to God the Father and his Son, Jesus! But as you begin to shout praise, a language you have never learned is coming out of your mouth! You normally speak Aramaic and a little Koine Greek, but this language is something you have never even heard before. All you know is that there is incredible joy and praise filling the air. You hear dozens of other languages being shouted by your friends. As a crowd gathers, someone calls out to you in Aramaic, "Hey, you speak my native language! You are praising God and speaking of the glories of Jesus of Nazareth!"

It's happened to you! You have received the power of the Spirit that Jesus promised, and you are indeed being a witness in a way that far exceeds your own ability. It's Acts 1:8 happening in real time.

Suddenly one of Jesus' closest friends, the disciple Peter, begins to preach to the crowd who has gathered. One of his themes is that what has happened to the people here is available to anyone who will repent and believe. Eight times he mentions, by word or concept, "all." This power is for "all" who are willing to receive it.

Speaking under the Spirit's power, Peter makes it unmistakably clear that this power is not limited to those gathered here or to the Jews or even to those alive at this time. Instead he says, "And you will receive the gift of the Holy Spirit. The promise is for you and your children and for all who are far off—for all whom the Lord our God will call" (Acts 2:38-39).

When I try to imagine that historical scene, I get "Holy Ghost goosebumps." But the best news is that the Spirit's fire is more alive than ever. There is a flame available for the head of every believer! Paul may have had this in mind when he wrote in 1 Thessalonians 5:19, "Do not quench the Spirit" or (as the ISV translation states) "Do not put out the Spirit's fire."

I believe God wants us to "claim our flame," to believe the power of his Spirit for carrying out his general and specific call on our lives. As Peter says in his Acts 2 sermon, "'In the last days, God says, I will pour out my Spirit on all people'" (v. 17).

Sadly, we settle for the "smoke" of the Christian religion instead of the "fire" of the Spirit's presence. We rely on the truth of the Bible for our creeds but not the power of the Spirit for our calling. We seek excuses and escape clauses rather than seeking the Spirit's assistance to do what we can't do on our own. We dumb down our calling to fit our ability or comfort zone. We create categories of Christians with a few special saints receiving the "real" power, while we get enough power to "get by"

… but not enough to "get going" to carry out God's real calling.

While we may not hear wind, see fire, or speak in unlearned languages, there is a supernatural dimension of power available and waiting to manifest through our lives and in our calling. Only our ignorance, neglect, apathy, unbelief, or fear is holding it back. We need to "claim the flame" of God's Spirit.

Sam Storms, author, pastor, and former president of the Evangelical Theological Society was a good friend of John Wimber, the founder of the Vineyard movement. Sam shares the following humorous but instructive story from John's ministry:

> John will be remembered for many things, one of which was his unrelenting commitment to "doin' the stuff," as he often put it. As John told the story, he and Carol visited a church early in his spiritual journey, immediately after he had spent considerable time reading the gospel accounts of the life and ministry of Jesus. Following the service, John approached the pastor and asked him: "So, when do we do the stuff?"
>
> "The stuff?" asked the pastor. "What's the 'stuff'?"
>
> "You know," John replied. "The stuff in the Bible, like healing the sick and casting out demons. The stuff!"
>
> "Oh," replied the pastor. "We don't do the stuff. We believe they did it back in biblical days, but we don't do it today."
>
> With a rather confused look on his face, John could only say: "And I gave up drugs for *this*?"[7]

Although John was a new believer without credentials of any kind, after reading the New Testament he wanted to "claim the flame" above his head. He wanted to "do the stuff." His expectations of God's power

---

[7] https://www.samstorms.org/all-articles/post/doin-the-stuff---remembering-john-wimber

were not grounded in his own identity but in the Spirit.

I love the fact that we don't know the names of the 72 missionaries Jesus sent out in Luke 10. What we do know is that Jesus gave them authority or power to heal the sick and cast out demons. This power wasn't just for the 12 apostles but for the unnamed followers of Jesus who were willing to carry out his mission.

The inclusive "allness" that Peter underlines in his first sermon should reverberate as a theme in our lives and ministries. We are included in this power promise, as is every "born from above" believer. There is indeed a flame available for every believer's head.

It is interesting, then, that the primary text for the priesthood of all believers flows from Peter—Peter, who preached at Pentecost (Acts 2); Peter, who saw the Spirit come upon the Gentile Cornelius and all his household (Acts 10). This man would be the one to most clearly articulate the calling of every believer to be a priest, a representative of God to the people who did not yet know him (see 1 Peter).

Peter's teaching of the priesthood of all believers has been recovered in principle but not in practice. Cultural Christians still want the professional Christians to do the work of ministry for them. That's what they pay their pastor to do. But Scripture declares a different call and power.

The priesthood of all believers flows from who Christ is. At Jesus' baptism, the Holy Spirit came upon Christ, anointing him as prophet, priest, and king (Luke 3:1-21; Matthew 3:1-17; Mark 1:1-11). Those in union with Christ participate in that same priestly anointing as demonstrated when the Father poured out his Spirit on the day of Pentecost (Acts 2:1-41).

Peter builds on this truth in 1 Peter 2 when he shows us that our priesthood flows from our connection to our high priest, Jesus. Through this union with Christ and sharing in his anointing, Peter can boldly declare, "You are a chosen race, a royal priesthood, a holy nation, a people for his own possession, that you may proclaim the excellencies of him who called you out of darkness into his marvelous light" (1 Peter 2:9, ESV).

The apostle John echoes and underlines this union with Christ, the source of our priesthood: "And they sang a new song, saying: 'You are worthy to take the scroll and to open its seals, because you were slain, and with your blood you purchased for God persons from every tribe and language and people and nation. You have made them to be a kingdom and priests to serve our God, and they will reign on the earth'" (Revelation 5:9-10).

John declares that the priestly salvific work of Jesus for people from every tribe, language, and nation not only saves them but anoints them to be priests who serve God. As many as are purchased by the blood of Christ have access to the anointing of Christ to be his priesthood. This is the empowered priesthood.

Return with me in your imagination to Pentecost as described at the start of this chapter. Fast forward with me from the start of Acts 2 to the end. After Peter's sermon you are there, praying in the common language of Aramaic with this diverse group of Jews who were repenting and believing upon Jesus as their risen Messiah. You go into the water and begin to help baptize lines of people declaring their allegiance to Christ.

The next days and weeks are a blur as you take some of your new friends under your spiritual wing and begin to disciple them. Some are locals; some are travelers who extended their stay to learn about their new faith. Soon you are leading a gathering in your house—a "house church" as part of the new church of Jerusalem.

Although you can't see the flame any longer, you feel its presence daily as you move in the new anointing of your priesthood. You are determined to "claim your flame" until Christ returns.

Your PMC is rooted in your priestly identity. As a royal priest, you can receive anointing and bless others with that anointing. You can speak *with* the living God, and you can speak *for* the living God to others. What you could never do on your own power becomes possible as your self-image is submitted to the thrilling reality of the Spirit's empowerment.

I have watched this happen through all kinds of ordinary people. When speaking at conferences on this topic, I often start with a riddle: What do a truck driver, a milk salesman, a convicted killer, a corporate business woman, a Korean rugby player, a Mexican cult member, a California beach girl, a Cambodian who escaped from the killing fields, a gang member with only an 8th-grade education, a COO of a corporation, a Kansas farm boy, and a construction worker have in common?

Answer: They have all planted churches out of our local church. They embraced the spiritual empowerment to be royal priests in the house of our God. The flame is for everyone. Are you ready to claim yours?

CHAPTER 3

Empowered Leadership—Are You a Leader or Follower?

"You are a leader!"

That statement is in quotations so you will know I am speaking directly to YOU ... but also because I am quoting what my pastor said to me when I was 16 years old. I had just finished preaching my first sermon (a train wreck of bad exegesis, exuberant teenage hubris, and a sincere heart of love). He looked in my eyes and said, "You are a leader."

I wasn't quite sure how to respond, so I stuttered out a confused, "Thank you." My next thought, which did not come out of my mouth was, "What do you mean, *leader*?"

When well-meaning people who we respect slap labels on our foreheads, it can be empowering and inspiring ... or it can be frightening, confusing, and even damaging.

I just did this to you. Without even knowing you, I audaciously declared you a leader! But I am not going to leave you with your feet dangling from the limb of ambiguity as to what that means.

"You are a leader."

I say that not because I know you, but because I know the One who lives in you. I understand (to a limited degree) the Holy Spirit's presence, power, and passions. I also know what the Bible states about your general and personal calling.

You might respond back to me, "But I want to be a follower, not a leader." I get that. Leading comes with responsibility. As Uncle Ben in *Spiderman* so accurately declared, "With great power comes great responsibility." Many Christians would certainly prefer lower power, lower responsibility. But is following without leading a viable option for a biblical Christian?

Following is a non-negotiable, an essential. In fact, it is the essence of our faith. Christians are followers. Seventeen times in the Gospels Jesus gives the invitation to "Follow me." Conversion is that commitment to stop following our own rationale and to start following God's truth. It demands a cessation of following self-will and embracing a lifestyle of following God's will.

Following Christ means to study with appreciation his ways of living and serving. To make every effort to imitate Jesus' values, attitudes, and actions. To discern what he said "No" to, and to say our "No" with him. To understand what he said "Yes" to, and to speak our affirmation in tandem with him.

But following Christ is more indirect than direct, meaning that (since he is not physically present) we follow those who teach us with their words and/or example what following Christ looks like. We follow Christian parents, teachers, authors, professors, friends, elders, pastors, and those with spiritual authority over us.

You cannot become a great leader without being an excellent follower. Empowered leaders are those who are close followers of those who are imitating Christ best. We see this principle in 1 Corinthians 11:1 when Paul states, "Follow my example, as I follow the example of Christ."

But being ONLY a follower is not an option that Jesus left open to us. He did not intend to. His mission was too vital and demanded that his followers become leaders.

"You are a leader."

Matthew 4:19 records Jesus' initial and overarching invitation, command, and promise: "Follow me ... and I will send you out to fish for people." As I like to say, "Good following always turns into good fishing!" Close following turns into good leading. But following that fails to result in leading is spiritually dysfunctional.

Leadership and Discipleship

"Not every Christian is a leader!" These were the words a gifted pastor of a significant church passionately challenged me with. Everyone in the group of pastors turned their eyes to me since (as the cohort leader) I was trying to convince them to more fully activate "the priesthood of all believers."

I replied, "The only way to discuss the validity of your statement is to agree on the definition of a leader."

This, of course, was a challenge because if you Google "leader," you find a plethora of definitions. So my approach was to move away from the term *leader* and move to Scripture.

So I asked, "Do you believe Jesus was speaking to all believers when he said, 'Go and make disciples' in Matthew 28:19?"

The pastor knew the obvious answer and couldn't deny the truth that disciple-making is God's call for every Christian. No matter how rare disciple-making is among American Christians, the fact remains that it is the invitation and expectation of Jesus for all his followers.

Then I inquired, "Is discipleship a form of leadership?" The answer was, "Again, it depends on your definition of leadership."

I said, "OK, let's move to perhaps the simplest definition of leadership available. One that is stated by Christian leadership expert, John Maxwell: 'Leadership is influence, nothing more, nothing less.'"[8]

So I continued, "Is discipleship a form of influence?" Of course. In fact, discipleship is the most valuable form of influence a person could ever engage in.

I understand why the pastor was pushing back against my statement. My leadership definition was built around a person-to-person influence, while his was built around the ability to influence a team or organization.

Not every Christian has the gifts or skills to cast vision, inspire participation, delegate positions, or organize and synchronize tasks to accomplish a mission. Romans 12:8 speaks of the gift of leadership, making it clear not all believers are "gifted to be leaders" in an organizational sense.

However, when we simplify "leadership" down to "discipleship," we discover that through the Spirit's power we are all empowered to exercise influence and lead people closer to Christ. I would argue that this is the most powerful form of leadership we can exercise.

There are other forms of valuable leadership within the Church, but biblical disciple-making is the most impactful. Here's why: Discipleship leadership releases an organic, primitive, unstoppable, multiplying force that can change the world.

---

8 https://www.johnmaxwell.com/blog/7-factors-that-influence-influence/

My pastor's declaration, "You are a leader," was empowering to me. I knew, however, that his words were more focused on my ability to speak and inspire than on my ability to disciple another person into the ways of Christ and teach them to repeat that with someone else.

For much of my ministry I majored in organizational and platform leadership and minored in discipleship. I was mistaken.

Similarly, for the past two decades the Church has carried on an affair with leadership—but strictly organizational leadership. This is reasonable, since the primary goal during this time has been church growth by addition. The larger a church or ministry in the church became, the more important the gift of leadership was. In those years I seldom heard the word *discipleship*, but I heard the cultural word *leadership* consistently. Yet, in the New Testament the word *disciple* or *disciples* is used approximately 300 times, while *leaders* is used 30 times, with 20 of those times being in a negative way.

Leonard Sweet recently gave this great image:

> Once upon a time, pastors had "studies." They would hunker down in their rooms surrounded by books to craft wonderful sermons. In the modern era, pastors have "offices" because we became pseudo CEO's that also manage staff and big budgets (we have to pay for that fancy entertainment each week!). After COVID-19, pastors are moving into "studios." Not just creative studios to produce our messages in video and podcast formats (which are great!), but studios in the vein of the old masters who had apprentice painters around them learning the craft and becoming better artists than their masters. That is the pastor's studio of tomorrow![9]

We need good organizational, church, group, and team leaders. But far more importantly we need for every believer to exercise the leadership

---

9 https://loganleadership.com/lessons-from-covid-19/

of discipleship with a few individuals who repeat that leadership with others. This multiplication discipleship approach has profound potential.

The following Kingdom multiplication math radically changed my ministry:

If an ordinary disciple trained one person for one year to be a disciple-maker who would repeat this process with someone else, the first year there would be two disciples. The second year, there would be four disciples becoming disciple-makers. Then, in the third year, those four disciples-makers would each take on another, making eight disciples.

This is slow but powerful Kingdom work. Don't quit. If you keep up the same pattern, in year four there are 16 disciples, then 32. By year six, you have 64 disciples in your generational downline. This is about the size of the average church in America. Keep making disciple-makers, and you'll have 128, then 256, 512, and 1,024. By year 11, you'll have 2,048 in your ministry legacy—the size of a megachurch!

Is that leadership? Amazing leadership! Yet, all you did was make one disciple a year who became a disciple-maker who repeated the process. This is why I am passionate about PMC and its potential Kingdom impact!

In my view, there are three primary obstacles that keep believers from stepping into their leadership call:

1. A shortage of **understanding** ... solved by learning the truth.

2. A shortage of **willingness** ... solved by a deepening of commitment.

3. A shortage of **power** ... solved by increasing their reception of the Spirit's power.

A lack of personal understanding is the first obstacle to empowered leadership. Most Christians and even a majority of pastors fail to understand God's calling on their lives.

Todd Wilson writes cogently on this calling in his excellent book *MORE,* in which he describes our lives as a rowboat with two oars. One oar represents disciple-making as the "general call" of God, incumbent upon *all* followers of Jesus. The other oar represents the "unique call" of God—a *personalized* commissioning based upon your context, gifts, strengths, talents, education, passions, and network. These two oars must be pulled on simultaneously, or the boat of your life will indefinitely circle aimlessly.

The second obstacle is willingness. Once a Christ follower *understands* God's true call on their life, they must face their own willingness to obey and to pursue that call. As Jesus so often pointed out, it is not the "hearing" but the "heeding" that matters. In John 14:21 Jesus tells us that the greater revelation of himself will come in response to our obedience to his commandments: "Whoever has my commands and keeps them is the one who loves me. The one who loves me will be loved by my Father, and I too will love them and show myself to them."

Our cultural Christianity has become so consumer oriented that we often act as if we can pick and choose which of Christ's commands look appetizing to us, as if we were at some sort of "command buffet." One of Christ's most important commands is found in the Great Commission (Matthew 28:19-20) and then again in his Acts 1:8 sending. But we treat these particular commands as dessert rather than as the main course. Our self-surrender to disciple-making must deepen, and our willingness to prioritize the mission over our comfort zone must increase.

Henry Blackaby speaks to this with these words: "The Holy Spirit doesn't need to equip you for what you're not going to do, so if you're in rebellion against Jesus and refusing His right to be Lord, He doesn't need to send the Holy Spirit to equip you for service. And, tragically, you miss out on the joy that He brings. So let the Holy Spirit deal with anything that's keeping you from obeying Christ."[10]

The third obstacle is key, and it impacts the first two: a shortage of power. We do not live Spirit-filled lives. Our engagement with the Holy Spirit is shallow and sporadic. We are operating on our own intellect, resolve, and strength instead of his. We are well-meaning but underpowered. We only attempt to do what we might be able to do in our own power.

The Spirit will almost daily ask us to do something beyond our own capability. (If we could do it in our own strength, we wouldn't need the Spirit's power.) The sad results are that we end up attempting far less than what we could for God, and when we *do* accomplish something good, we accept some of the applause. But the power of the *Spirit* will lead us *beyond* our own strength and reveal God's presence in such a way that only he receives the glory.

We must learn to grow in our calling as empowered leaders.

---

10 https://www.goodreads.com/author/quotes/21025.Henry_T_Blackaby

CHAPTER 4

The Position of Empowerment— Suntans and Rivers

My guess is that you wouldn't be reading this book if you didn't desire to live a more spirit-empowered life. This brings the question, *Whose responsibility is your current power level?* Is your empowerment level due to God choosing to withhold his power, or is it due to something in your life that is out of alignment? Is there a position you can take to dramatically influence your power level?

John 3:34 is both a description of how Jesus lived and an invitation to how we can live. "For the one whom God has sent speaks the words of God, for God gives the Spirit without limit." God is not the cause for any limitations of the Spirit we may be experiencing. God's desire is to fill us daily with his Spirit.

Then why is there such a power shortage in our lives? Positioning.

We don't earn power, or deserve power, or demand power, or achieve power. We *receive* power. But we must position ourselves to receive this power. In his humanity, Jesus lived in a position to receive the fullness of the Spirit daily. He is the model for those of us who would live empowered.

If you live in Phoenix, you can have a suntan all year long if you'd like. Why? Because 86% of the days are sunny there. In suntanning, the sun does all the work. You can't make the sun shine. Your responsibility is to position yourself so the sun has access to you. If you never go outdoors, or if you spend your life under an umbrella, you will be as pale as a Seattleite.

My personal ministry story reveals this reality. Skipping the middle of the story (which I will share later), I had become a success in the eyes of the church world and had privately decided that my next big step would be to pursue my doctorate degree. I wanted to learn more about how to lead even bigger and better organizations. The only question was where I should go to get my doctorate.

I didn't realize it, but I was trying to be a "Martha," serving Jesus better and serving more people better. But I was missing what was *truly* better. I was missing a "Mary" lifestyle (see Luke 10:38-42). As the cliche says, I had a "passion for the work of the Lord but not the Lord of the work." I was working *for* the sixth day, instead of working *from* the seventh day.

As a result, I was relying more and more on my own determination, motivation, and self-sufficiency. This resulted in a sporadic drought in my spiritual vibrancy and internal satisfaction. A performance-based identity had dried up much of the joy of my salvation. The mission was a duty, more than a delight.

But the Spirit broke through in an odd way. One morning at about 8 a.m. I was on my knees beside my bed asking God, "Where do you want me to do my doctoral work? What kind of doctorate do you want me to pursue? Who are the teachers you want me to learn from?" Unexpectedly, I heard the door of our mail slot open and close. I thought it was undoubtedly a solicitor passing out the latest invitation to try their new restaurant. It was far too early for the mail to arrive.

Curious, I went to our mail slot and pulled out a half-page typed letter addressed to me. I ran to the door to see who had left it, but no one was there to be seen. As I began to read the letter, goosebumps went up my spine. In essence the letter said, "As I was praying this morning, the Lord gave me a strong prophecy concerning you. You are making a major decision today, and you need to prioritize that which will bring you closer to Jesus, not that which will elevate you in the eyes of others. Sit at the feet of Jesus, and you will receive all that you really need."

No one knew of the decision I was contemplating, but the Lord wrote me a letter through a willing servant. My tendency to be a type A leader who ran hard and measured my worth by visible successes was being addressed by the Holy Spirit himself. Of the four programs I was considering, three of them were in leadership, and one was in spiritual formation.

I would go on to receive a Doctorate of Ministry with an emphasis in spiritual formation and learn from professors such as Richard Foster, Dallas Willard, Maxie Dunnam, and many other wisdom-filled Christian thinkers and leaders. I leaned into the "Mary" lifestyle, and (though I still have my "Martha" moments) I am a deeper, more satisfied, peace-filled, and empowered leader than I ever was before.

What happened to me? I began to prioritize positioning myself to be in his presence. The empowered person learns how to position themselves daily so the Spirit will have the fullest access to their lives.

Scriptures enlighten us about this type of positioning using four water metaphors:

Psalm 1:3 makes a promise based on positioning: "That person is like a tree planted by streams of water, which yields its fruit in season and whose leaf does not wither—whatever they do prospers." In the arid topography of Palestine, the closer a tree is planted to a stream, the more fruitful and drought-resistant it will be. The psalmist likens us to trees that get to choose where they plant themselves. The water is available to all, but some will position themselves nearer and some further from it. The fruit will be borne accordingly.

Ezekiel 47:1-12 is another water metaphor, but this picture calls us to position ourselves deeper in the river. The angel shows Ezekiel a trickle of water flowing from the temple, then leads Ezekiel downriver. The further they go, the deeper the water. At first the water is ankle-deep, then knee deep, then waist deep, then deep enough to swim in. At this point the current of the river is deep enough and strong enough to carry the prophet along in its power. But also the further he went downriver, the more fruit trees and fish there were.

Believers position themselves at different depths in the river. Some stop at the ankle-deep water of salvation. Others are willing to go knee deep serving in the church. Some will even go waist deep in the water of missional living. But as long as their feet are still on the bottom, they are in control. Few will go deep enough to surrender control to where the river current carries them along. They are living in the current of the Spirit. It is this position that carries them to the life of empowerment, enjoyment, and lasting fruitfulness they truly yearn for. I want to be in over my head, and I think you do as well. It's about positioning.

Jesus picks up on this water, river, and flowing metaphor in **John 7:37-39**: "On the last and greatest day of the festival, Jesus stood and said in a loud voice, 'Let anyone who is thirsty come to me and drink.

Whoever believes in me, as Scripture has said, rivers of living water will flow from within them.'" By *living water* he meant the Spirit.

The invitation Jesus makes is two-fold: 1) Come to me, and 2) Drink from me. These are the two key aspects of positioning for us. The first can speak of our *attitudes*, and the second of our *actions*. There are attitudes that bring us to the Spirit and open us to the Spirit. There are actions that are used to receive the water, to intake the water from the river into our lives.

God uses the picture of a spring of water to underscore the criticalness of these attitudes in **Proverbs 4:23**: "Above all else, guard your heart, for everything you do flows from it." The heart position of a person either blocks or releases the flow of God's Spirit into them and through them.

Attitudes of the heart aren't complete without actions of the head and the hands. These spiritual habits or activities create pipelines for the power of God to flow from his divine Spirit into our human souls.

Paul exhorts Timothy of this holy combination. "Train yourself to be godly. … Be diligent in these matters; give yourself wholly to them, so that everyone may see your progress" (1 Timothy 4:7b, 15). This training positions you for godliness. Diligence in spiritual actions enables others to see true progress in your power and fruitfulness levels.

The Spirit is more than willing and available. The question is, are *we* willing and available? Will spiritual positioning become the daily priority of our lives?

The next few chapters share some of these key attitudes and actions that position us for these greater levels of empowerment.

CHAPTER 5

The Seat of Empowerment—
The Best Seat in the House

I was brand new on the board of a very large Christian university. At a commencement with several thousand people, I ended up in the front of the trustees line to enter the event. I mistakenly thought all the trustees sat on the platform in the chairs of honor. Consequently, I started to march up onto the platform not realizing that we were seated on the floor of the auditorium, not the stage. An usher redirected me back to the floor, and I prayed for the rapture to rescue me from my deep embarrassment.

The power dynamics of the Kingdom of God are upside-down from the kingdom of the world. In the world, the most powerful seat is the one nearest the front. This creates a scramble to sit at the head table, where you can be known, honored, positioned by people. Celebrities sit up front. Servants sit in the back.

But Jesus told a story to identify the power seat in his Kingdom. I encourage you to read it aloud, slowly, visualizing yourself as a guest at the banquet. Try to feel the emotions and thoughts you might have as you: 1) select a seat, 2) watch people come in and size them up, 3) are asked to move back, and 4) are asked to move up.

> When he noticed how the guests picked the places of honor at the table, he told them this parable: "When someone invites you to a wedding feast, do not take the place of honor, for a person more distinguished than you may have been invited. If so, the host who invited both of you will come and say to you, 'Give this person your seat.' Then, humiliated, you will have to take the least important place. But when you are invited, take the lowest place, so that when your host comes, he will say to you, 'Friend, move up to a better place.' Then you will be honored in the presence of all the other guests. For all those who exalt themselves will be humbled, and those who humble themselves will be exalted" (Luke 14:7-11).

If we want to be truly empowered, we must learn to love sitting in the back with the servants. Jesus powerfully taught and modeled this position: "For even the Son of Man did not come to be served, but to serve" (Mark 10:45). Spiritual empowerment requires attitudes that attract the Spirit.

A mentor told me, "Larry, remember the water of the Spirit always flows to the lowest place. If you get low, his Spirit will flow. So face on the floor and exalt him more." This seat of humility is not a place of personal diminishment or self-flagellation but a place of confidence, service, contribution, and trust.

Confidence: We are confident in who we are in Christ; therefore, we don't need to sit up front to prove we are special.

Service: We are asking how we can help, not how we can be heard or seen.

Contribution: We may sit down in back, but we speak up when we have something to contribute because we are unafraid of the opinions of others.

Trust: We know the Master will call us forward, if and when he wants us there. We trust him to assign us our seats instead of deciding our own seating chart.

For the last 50 years especially there has been a scramble for Christian notoriety. With the rise of the publishing, broadcasting, conferences, megachurches, and internet industries, the rush for the seats up front has accelerated. These industries have all majored in addition—focusing on the number of people served, not the number of people serving.

A quest for the glory of addition, to quickly build something big, has obstructed the power of multiplication, which demands thinking "few" and long.

Jesus worked in the opposite direction of the world. He understood that if he could sit in the back and disciple a few to join him there, he could start a multiplication movement that would change the world. He welcomed the crowds, but he prioritized the few. This demanded "lower seat" thinking.

This is why Jesus washed his disciples' feet then instructed them to go and do to others what he had done for them. Multiply yourselves through your humility of service. His Kingdom's flag would be a servant's towel (John 13:13-17).

We too quickly run to the front, to the appearance of power and run past the seats of true spiritual power. Or we seek to leverage spiritual power for self-advancement. We deploy our gifts to take us to seats where our character cannot sustain us. This is the danger of discounting the seats in the back. We have seen the spiritual carnage to individuals, families, churches, and the Kingdom due to this deception.

Empowerment increases the more fully we lean into Jesus' vine-and-branch wisdom. Jesus actually meant it when he said, "Apart from me you can do nothing" (John 15:5). We can grow "fake fruit" on our own, but Jesus was describing "fruit that will last" (v. 16). Fruit "lasts" when it reproduces and multiplies. This demands the attitude of complete dependence and humility. I cannot simultaneously be depending on the Spirit and myself.

Jesus has one other teaching on seats and attitudes. It is a radical teaching that grates against the nerves of self-focused leaders (like I can too often be).

> "Suppose one of you has a servant plowing or looking after the sheep. Will he say to the servant when he comes in from the field, 'Come along now and sit down to eat'? Won't he rather say, 'Prepare my supper, get yourself ready and wait on me while I eat and drink; after that you may eat and drink'? Will he thank the servant because he did what he was told to do? So you also, when you have done everything you were told to do, should say, 'We are unworthy servants; we have only done our duty'" (Luke 17:7-10).

This story undermines our desire to get the credit for our labor. We want a master who will give us applause for our efforts. We believe we deserve to sit at the table because we have worked so hard. Yet, Jesus points us to the seat in the back. We don't understand the privilege of serving, the mercy of even being in the Master's house, or the reward that obedience itself really is.

The old maxim, "It is amazing how much can be accomplished when no one cares who gets the credit" finds its roots here. When we find ourselves desiring the credit, feeling we deserve the seats up front, we must stop and check our humility gauge.

In January of 2021 we handed the keys of the church we had pastored for 31 years over to the two new co-lead pastors we had raised up. Then we left for six weeks on ministry and personal trips. When I came back to our church for a Sunday service, I arrived early and was greeted at the door by someone I had never seen. They welcomed me and asked, "Is this your first time?" I replied, "No, actually I've been here before."

Then I was ushered in by another new person. They led me to a seat in the middle of the sanctuary. They asked, "Is this good for you?" I answered, "Yes, this will do fine," while inside I was hurt and thinking, "After 31 years of sitting in the front row, I'm gone for six weeks, and I'm forgotten?"

Then the Spirit reminded me of these two stories that Jesus told, and I was convicted. Had I served such a long time so I could stay seated on the front row? Or had I served because the Master is worthy of all my life, and he alone deserves to be exalted? Would I be content to serve wholeheartedly if I was never "seen"? (Full disclosure—when the new pastors came in, they promptly came and moved me to the front row and asked me to always sit there.)

But true humility is living in agreement with God about who I really am. This both lowers and raises us into all we can be. This is the seat of power. If we are going to raise the y score of our empowerment level, it will always begin by lowering ourselves and choosing the best seat in the house!

CHAPTER 6
The Expectation of Empowerment—Faithing Your Future

I love seeing miracles happen in response to prayer—especially the instantaneous ones that are undeniably God-caused. I remember one of our mission teams in the Philippines praying for a man who had been in a wheelchair for several years. At the conclusion of us anointing and praying for him, he stood up on atrophied legs and began to walk.

This was not a "made for TV" moment, where the cameras worked their deceptive power; it was the real deal. In fact, the next evening he and his wife were there in the service, standing and praising God. His wife shared with all of us that she had awakened that morning to strange noises in her kitchen only to find her husband standing at the stove making her breakfast for the first time in seven years.

The bigger miracle happened that evening when the man received Christ as Savior and was born again. This far more important miracle of eternal consequence was accompanied with no outwardly observable signs.

I immediately recalled Jesus' words to his 72 disciples in Luke 10.

They returned exclaiming about the healings and deliverances they had observed. It is almost as if Jesus replied, "What did you expect?" Jesus says, "Of course my power worked. I have empowered you with authority." But then Jesus redirects: "However, do not rejoice that the spirits submit to you, but rejoice that your names are written in heaven" (Luke 10:20).

The reality of the gospel changing the eternal destination of a soul is by far the greater miracle. It is the great true story that has changed our story. It is the story we carry as a gift to offer to others. But the question is: "What do we expect?"

Every empowered person we see in the biblical story is noted for faith. From salvation to miracles to multiplication, these graces are received through faith, through an expectation of God to keep his word. Empowerment begins with expectation.

I call it "Faithing our future," believing that what's ahead can be better than what's behind. It is imagining the future based on God's power. Paul prays forward with faith, and we need to make his prayer our posture daily: "Now to him who is able to do immeasurably more than all we ask or imagine, according to his power that is at work within us, to him be glory in the church and in Christ Jesus throughout all generations, for ever and ever! Amen" (Ephesians 3:20-21).

Sadly, our familiarity with Jesus has diminished our faith, and consequently we will miss the fullness of the future God wants for us. The manifestations of his power await an environment of faith to be released. Many Christian leaders suffer from what I call the "Nazareth Syndrome."

Jesus had been healing the sick, casting out demons, and proclaiming the good news of the Kingdom throughout Galilee (Matthew 11:5).

Now he returns to his hometown of Nazareth and ministers in the synagogue. The people are trying to align what they have recently heard about Jesus with the man they have known for years. Jesus was commonplace to them. Their expectations had been shaped by their past encounters.

The result of this attitude? "And he did not do many miracles there because of their lack of faith" (Matthew 13:58). **The power they experienced *from* Jesus was based on their expectations *of* him.** The same will be true for us.

The power we receive from God, whether for salvation, miracles, or multiplication, is directly connected to our faith. It is our expectation of what God *will* do, not just what God *can* do, that unleashes the manifestation of his power in us and through us.

Too often we suffer from Nazareth Syndrome. Like those in Nazareth, we have tamed the great Lion of Judah with our unbelief. Our small expectations of his power lead us to efforts more akin to Amway than to the One who is "The Way." Our faith is in propositional truth alone instead of also being in the person who is "The Truth." The propositions secure us, but they do not surprise us. Jesus, however, is always ready to do the unexpected and the undeserved *if* we will exercise our faith.

Paul wrote to the Christians at Corinth: "My message and my preaching were not with wise and persuasive words, but with a demonstration of the Spirit's power, so that your faith might not rest on human wisdom, but on God's power" (1 Corinthians 2:4-5). Do we expect God's power to be at work in unexpected ways so that we minister with both truth *and* power?

Brian Warth was serving a life sentence that started at age 16 when Jesus unexpectedly showed up through some of his servants. Brian not only was saved, but he was called into ministry. His sentence was miraculously commuted 17 years later, and he was released on parole. So I hired him to plant a church, and some of our church people shook their heads at me.

But I saw a fire on Brian's head. Brian had a faith in God to be God in his life and in his ministry. Brian expected his church plant to not just survive but to grow and multiply. Eight years later, Chapel of Change was a thriving church of 1,000 that had already planted two churches.

It took *more* than faith, but it *started* with faith. The same will be true for you—if you expect it.

CHAPTER 7

The Air of Empowerment—Breathing Well

I learned to pray from Harold. I never asked him where he learned. Harold was actually Pastor Taves (who I wrote about earlier), pastor of Ulysses First Church of God, a church of a few dozen believers in my small farming town. Harold didn't teach me to pray through lectures *on* prayer but through sharing his life *of* prayer.

I was Harold's apprentice during my senior year of high school. This meant I got out of school for half a day, every day, to spend time with Harold. A portion of every afternoon was spent with the two of us all alone in the church sanctuary, kneeling at the altar, praying for the church. At first I thought that we should be doing something more "productive," but I didn't realize how much my young energy needed to be supplemented by real spiritual empowerment.

Harold was stricken with polio at a young age. For the rest of his life, he was unable to lift his left arm more than a few inches. Yet, my most vivid memory of Harold was with his right arm stretched up to Heaven as he interceded for God's work in our church and town. To this day,

Harold was one of the most empowered people I have ever met.

Prayer and power are the lungs-and-air relationship of the spiritual realm. Prayer receives and processes the air or breath of the Spirit. The Greek word for Spirit is *pneuma*, which comes from the root word *pneo*, meaning "to breathe" or "to blow." It should not surprise us, then, that when the Spirit was first poured out, the manifestation was "a sound like a mighty rushing wind" (Acts 2:2, ESV).

Take three long, slow, deep breaths. If you did so (instead of just reading it), you had to focus, to concentrate. But before that, you were breathing without thinking, the way you live through every day. This is the call of prayer: learning to pray your way through the day, learning to breathe well. Sometimes you intensely focus; other times you are unconsciously lifting your spirit to the Holy Spirit. Often this manifests itself in "breath prayers." One of the breath prayers I pray through the day is "Spirit, fill me now."

Prayer and power integrate so completely that it's hard to even think of being empowered to empower others without the connection to prayer. After all, Jesus picked his first disciples after a night of prayer (Luke 6:12-13). The first church was born in a prayer meeting (Acts 1-2). And the first recorded church planting movement started from fasting and prayer (Acts 13:1-3).

Some of you might be yawning right now thinking, "Why do I need to read a chapter on prayer? I know prayer is important." But the distance between prayer as a method and prayer as a lifestyle is deceptive—it's like the mirage that seems so near and satisfying, yet it is never reached. When prayer is a chore to accomplish or a timesheet to be filled in, it is no longer a privilege to enjoy and employ throughout the day, and it quickly loses its Empowerment Factor.

There are three forms of prayer that invite the fullness of the Spirit's empowerment: identification, integrated, and intervening.

Identification Prayer

This is the prayer that shapes our personal identity at the deepest level. Identification prayer is summed up in the words of a fellow pastor who daily prayed something like this: "Lord, put your fingers deep into the clay of my life today. Find the hard spots and soften them. Find the rough spots and smooth them. Shape me so that others see more of you in me. As Adam was molded, mold me until I hear you say, 'Very good.' Thank you that my identity is found in whose hands I am in."

This type of ongoing conversation with God addresses our darkest fears, our ugliest insecurities, our impurest motives, and our most stubborn doubts. It confronts our false need for success, the limiting lies we have believed, and the untrue emotions that hobble us.

But it also reveals the glory of God within us, the beauty and strength he created us with, the spiritual gifts he has bestowed upon us, the wisdom we possess through his Word and Spirit, and the authority we walk in as his children.

This kind of prayer happens in the teachable moments of ordinary days. It especially occurs in solitude as we speak authentically of our thoughts and feelings. We wait in the presence of God with an ear tuned to his voice. We come as we are—no pretense, agenda, façade, or guardedness. Openness, transparency, and vulnerability invite engagement and intimacy with the Father.

Eighteenth-century Archbishop François Fénelon described prayer this way:

> Tell God all that is in your heart, as one unloads one's heart, its pleasures and its pains, to a dear friend. Tell God your troubles,

that God may comfort you; tell God your joys, that God may sober them; tell God your longings, that God may purify them; tell God your dislikes, that God may help you conquer them; talk to God of your temptations, that God may shield you from them; show God the wounds of your heart, that God may heal them. If you thus pour out all your weaknesses, needs, troubles, there will be no lack of what to say. Talk out of the abundance of the heart, without consideration say just what you think. Blessed are they who attain to such familiar, unreserved intercourse with God.[11]

Did you read Fénelon's words slowly enough to let them shape how you pray? If not, slow down and read it aloud, so you hear yourself talk to yourself about your prayer life.

This type of transparency and constancy in prayer increases our intimacy with Christ and our potency for Christ. This is why one of my ongoing daily prayers is: "Lord, tell me the truth about me."

The more secure we are in who *we* are in Christ, the more empowered we are to let others know who *they* really are. We no longer compete and compare; instead we bless and rejoice. Our insecurities no longer hold us back in fear, nor do they thrust us forward in pride.

Lloyd Ogilvie, former chaplain of the US Senate, was the one who introduced me to identity prayer. At our college chapel, Ogilvie paused dramatically and allowed the room to grow silent. Then he said, "This is a holy moment as I want to share my life's prayer with you. It has transformed my life and directed my personal quest." I had my pen ready as he prayed the words: "Lord, make my life as beautiful as it was when you first thought about me!"

---

11   James Mudge, "Fénelon the Mystic," 1906. Online version available at the Christian History Institute online. http://chi.gospelcom.net/pastwords/chl175.shtml (accessed February 2007).

That was it. Simple but profound. Short but empowering. God's design for you was a life of full empowerment by his Spirit. To be shaped through prayer into the original design God intended is a journey that leads to increasing and true effectiveness.

Integrated Prayer

For prayer to shape a pastor's life and ministry, it must be woven into the fabric of daily life. It is integrated into the ordinary routine and unusual moments of life.

Prayer is not something the empowered disciple does only in order to prepare for the day—it is the means by which they travel through the day. Integrated prayer is a running conversation with God that begins on waking and ends on the pillow at night. It prioritizes and enjoys Paul's admonition, "Don't worry about anything; instead, pray about everything" (Philippians 4:6, TLB).

Archbishop Fénelon understood integrated prayer when he wrote, "Accustom yourself gradually to carry prayer into all your daily occupation—speak, act, work in peace, as if you were in prayer, as indeed you ought to be."[12] He knew that this attitude of prayer has transforming power. Integrating prayer into the minutiae of life brings a sense of significance, satisfaction, and holiness to the most humdrum tasks of life, work, and ministry.

My best days combine what I call "focused" and "fellowship" prayer. Focused prayer is when I set aside a time to bless the Lord for who he is, repent for shortcomings, intercede for others, and intentionally look ahead at my day to unleash the power of prayer on those problems and possibilities. But fellowship prayer is a means of integrating a conversation based on what happens inside me and around me as I travel through the day.

---

12 James Mudge, "Fénelon the Mystic," 1906.

Many pastors enter ministry with unrealistic expectations of amazing Sundays of impact and weeks filled with study, prayer, and teaching. Upon arrival at their first post, however, they can relate to Brother Lawrence, the sixteenth-century monk who found that peeling potatoes and washing dirty dishes were the unsavory realities of his daily ministry chores. Brother Lawrence complained for an entire decade before beginning to "practice the presence of God" and eventually write about it.

Four centuries later, we are still buying his classic book, *The Practice of the Presence of God*. Why is it such an enduring bestseller? As Brother Lawrence himself said, "There is not in the world a kind of life more sweet and delightful than that of a continual conversation with God."[13] He learned to peel his potatoes for the glory of God, enjoying the presence of God. Effectiveness is not measured by how fast a pastor can escape ministry tasks that seem below their expensive seminary training, but by how thoroughly they can integrate prayer into the unpleasant or mundane chores of ministry.

Integrated prayer ties the loose ends of ministry together—it gives some order to the chaos of ministry. It brings together seemingly unrelated events and identifies common threads so that spiritual understanding results. We lay the variety of puzzle pieces before God and say, "Lord, I trust you to make sense of it all."

Integrated prayer operates like a gyroscope, a device for maintaining orientation. It continuously revolves around every circumstance to keep the believer centered and stabilized. When journeying in prayer, the Christian can keep their bearings while navigating the maze of ministry and life.

---

13 https://ccel.org/ccel/lawrence/practice/practice.iv.v.html, Accessed October 23, 2023.

Intervening Prayer

The privilege of prayer is a delegated authority for the disciples of Jesus to interrupt the reign of evil and to extend the Kingdom of God. The ability of the believer to change the spiritual atmosphere of a situation through prayer must never be underestimated.

An old cartoon shows a pastor on his knees deep in prayer. His assistant opens the door and, upon seeing the pastor in prayer, exclaims, "Good, I am glad you're not busy!" This attitude is sadly all too common. Prayer is often seen as an escape from the "real" work of ministry, rather than an engagement in the most important work of ministry.

But the apostle James reminds us that "the prayer of a righteous person is powerful and effective" (James 5:16). A prayer of faith impacts the spiritual realm in Heaven and the reality here on earth, and it results in increased effectiveness. It intervenes.

Christians often pray as thermometers instead of thermostats. Like thermometers, their prayers reflect the reality of life—they praise God for what is, or they complain to God about what is not. Thermostats, on the other hand, monitor the temperature and intervene. They draw on the power of the furnace to heat the room. They change the atmosphere.

One National Day of Prayer, I felt directed by the Holy Spirit to do something totally uncharacteristic of my usual pattern. A busy intersection near our urban church had been the site of three robbery-homicides over the previous year, and the Lord prompted me to spend the day prayer-walking that corner, carrying a sign that read "National Day of Prayer: Praying for Peace in Our Neighborhood." As I did this, I was joined by others from our church. We received everything from honks of support to mock drive-by shootings, but we sensed the Spirit changing the atmosphere through our authoritative prayers.

A year later, at that corner three new businesses had opened, the closed business had reopened, and there had not been one robbery or murder. I believe our prayers changed the atmosphere of that street corner. Authoritative, intervening prayer can change the corners in your world, too.

If we want to live with a high *y* (an elevated empowered score), we must make prayer as common and as near as the air we breathe. We must live in a cadence of exhaling, "I release myself, my sin, my needs, my concerns" and inhaling, "I receive your Spirit to forgive, to fill, to guide, to satisfy, to bear fruit, to intervene, to empower."

CHAPTER 8

The Words of Empowerment— Power Bread

If you are near my age, you grew up in the 1960s watching Wonder Bread commercials. Their famous mantra was "Helps build strong bodies 12 ways." The truth is, you would consume less sugar by eating a Dum Dum Lollipop than two slices of Wonder Bread.

As fallen humans, we desire what immediately tastes good more than what will truly empower us. I used to love Wonder Bread, but now it sounds disgusting to me. I have developed a taste (sometimes even a craving for) the heavy, whole grain with seeds, no sugar kind of bread. It actually *does* build strong bodies.

Empowerment comes when the living Word of God becomes life-giving to us. When the words of truth and love are breathed into our spirits, our minds, and our hearts. It is Power Bread.

(Warning: In these days of instant online chats, texts, emails, FaceTime, and Zoom, the next two paragraphs will be hard to understand.)

The lovingly sculpted cursive on the page also carried a fragrance of her perfume. It was a long awaited letter from my high school girlfriend who had moved to Guam (about the furthest a place could be from our farm house in Kansas). Her affectionate words created an inexplicable yearning in my immature heart that literally left me without an appetite. I must have reread them a hundred times. Her heart was in those words.

I had never known words on a page could have such power. At that point I would have climbed any mountain, swam any ocean, traversed any valley to be with her. Although puppy love dies easily and we eventually broke up, I never forgot the force of her love letters from Guam.

I have occasionally reflected on that experience when I approach God's love letter to us—not the immaturity of fleeting adolescent romantic emotions, but the power of words to carry the heart of a person in such a way that I am empowered into action.

Most Christians read the Bible to gain meaning from the words—and that is necessary, noble, and helpful. But empowered Christians are looking for something more; they are looking to receive the marrow in the bone, the life in the letters, the Spirit in the words, the heart of Christ.

This is what Jesus offers us in his words: "The Spirit gives life; the flesh counts for nothing. The words I have spoken to you—they are full of the Spirit and life" (John 6:63). If *we* would be full of the Spirit, we must fill ourselves with the *words* that are "full of the Spirit."

We must approach the words of Scripture far differently than we do any other words. If we do not, then we risk being deceived like the Pharisees. They were in the right book looking for the wrong thing. They were seeking life from the words, but the words were pointing to the One who called himself "the Life" (John 14:6). Jesus rebuked them: "You study the Scriptures diligently because you think that in them you have eternal life. These are the very Scriptures that testify about me, yet you refuse to come to me to have life" (John 5:39-40).

The words of the Bible are pointing us to the life found only in Christ. Scriptures are filled with the Spirit of Christ. We must read them not only to know the truth but to encounter the One who *is* the Truth. We must be on guard, lest we are "always learning but never able to come to a knowledge of the truth" (2 Timothy 3:7) and end up "having a form of godliness but denying its power" (v. 5).

Jesus likened God's Word to daily bread when he said, "It is written: 'Man shall not live on bread alone, but on every word that comes from the mouth of God'" (Matthew 4:4). Later, he declared, "I am the bread of life. Whoever comes to me will never go hungry" (John 6:35).

Hungry people get power from eating bread, not just admiring it.

David and his team were ravenously hungry when David showed up to the tabernacle at Nob asking Ahimelek, the priest, for food (1 Samuel 21:1-6). The bread of the Presence used for worship was all Ahimelek had. In essence, David said, "Holy bread won't help us unless we eat it."

I had a friend named Ken in college who knew the Bible better than anyone I had ever met. We called him the "Bible Machine." If you asked him anything, anywhere in the Bible, he could tell you about it. He put a lot of Bible into his brain but never put a lot of Jesus into his life. No one I know of was attracted to Jesus through Ken. Sadly, a few years later I heard that Ken was no longer walking with Jesus.

Our hunger must be for the Bread of Life in the "words of life." Ezekiel, Jeremiah, and John the apostle are all recorded as having "eaten" the Word. I pray frequently for Jeremiah's experience of the Word. "When your words came, I ate them; they were my joy and my heart's delight, for I bear your name, Lord God Almighty" (Jeremiah 15:16).

I have done one 40-day fast. It was tough and empowering. The only chewable thing on my fast was the communion bread served each Sunday at our church. I would choose the largest broken piece of matzah in the plate and then go back through the line several times. While that last sentence is slightly exaggerated, I did crave this communion bread. That yearning led me to a new prayer, "Lord, I want this depth of craving for your Word."

The practice of *Lectio Divina* can help us "eat" the Word and derive life from it.

My modified practice of *Lectio Divina* involves six movements:

1. **Opening prayer:** posturing the heart to receive the Spirit in the Word

2. **Reading:** a slow, phrase-by-phrase reading of a small portion of Scripture

3. **Listening prayer:** hearing what the Spirit is saying to me personally in the Word

4. **Meditation:** engaging the mind to think deeply and repeatedly on the truth revealed

5. **Contemplation:** engaging the heart to experience God in the words, resting silently in their truth and love

6. **Submission:** listening for anything the Spirit would tell me to take action upon and committing myself to go and obey.

Our empowerment levels do not rise based on the number of verses we read or consecutive days of having a daily devotion. We are empowered by consistent engagement with the Spirit of God through the Word of God. His divine words of love can repeatedly set our hearts aflame unlike any human words ever could.

CHAPTER 9

The Habits of Empowerment— The Dance of Discipline

One of the most truthful quotes I've ever heard is, "First you make your habits, then your habits make you." Nineteenth-century theologian Nathanael Emmons wrote, "Habit is either the best of servants, or the worst of masters."[14]

Habits are an acquired behavior pattern regularly followed until it has become almost involuntary.[15] According to a recent study, a daily action like eating fruit at lunch or running for 15 minutes took an average of 66 days to become as much of a habit as it would ever become.[16]

The development of our own habits is the crucible for learning to lead. Our habits are the demonstration of our true priorities. They deepen the authenticity of our leadership efforts.

Former CEO, Harvard Professor of Leadership, and author Bill George

---

14 https://quotation.io/page/quote/habit-either-best-servants-worst-masters
15 https://www.dictionary.com/browse/habit Accessed July 17, 2021.
16 https://www.psychologytoday.com/us/blog/the-happiness-project/200910/stop-expecting-change-your-habit-in-21-days Accessed July 17, 2021.

states, "Leadership is not exerting power over others or exhorting them to follow you. Rather, it results from your example of empowering others to step up and lead. Leaders do that by learning to lead themselves, becoming self-aware and behaving authentically."[17]

The "training" the apostle Paul exhorted us to do in 1 Timothy 4:7 was undoubtedly a development of habits that led to godliness.

Dallas Willard captures this truth most brilliantly when he writes:

> The path of spiritual growth in the riches of Christ is not a passive one. Grace is not opposed to effort. It is opposed to earning. Effort is action. Earning is attitude. You have never seen people more active than those who have been set on fire by the grace of God. Paul, who perhaps understood grace better than any other mere human being, looked back at what had happened to him and said: "By the grace of God I am what I am, and his grace toward me did not prove vain; but I labored even more than all of them, yet not I, but the grace of God with me" (1 Corinthians 15:10, LSB).

As to "means of grace" placed in our hands, well-directed action is the key. The disciplines of the spiritual life are simply practices that prove to be effectual in enabling us to increase the grace of God in our lives.[18]

We who want to grow in our empowerment levels must intentionally choose "well-directed actions" repeatedly until habits are developed that create sustained spiritual momentum in our lives.

Novelty is not the aim in these habits, but personalization certainly is. We look back through the centuries to those who have gone before us to observe and learn from their flame-stoking disciplines. We look

---

17 https://www.billgeorge.org/page/leadership-skills-start-with-self-awareness/ Accessed July 19, 2021.

18 https://dwillard.org/articles/live-life-to-the-full. Accessed January 26, 2021.

ultimately to Jesus to pattern our lives after his spiritual practices.

First, we prioritize those habits that are most helpful to us personally. These are the practices that make "our heart sing" when we engage in them. Then, we look for the habits that are most difficult for us. These are usually those that address our weaknesses instead of our strengths.

Gary Thomas, author of *Sacred Pathways—Nine Ways to Connect with God*, unpacks nine different spiritual temperaments that are helpful for many, including me.[19] These nine are not an exhaustive list but a solid representation of the most common types of engagement with the Spirit. The following is my own paraphrased list based on Gary Thomas' work. Which temperaments resonate most strongly with you?

Naturalists connect with God in his creation. Sky, grass, flowers, trees, mountains, waters, etc. are a medium for naturalists to experience God's presence.

Intellectuals find refueling in books and concepts. They want to *learn* something, not just feel something.

Sensates plug in best through sights, sounds, smells, touches, and tastes. Art, music, architecture, foods, fabrics, etc. stoke their fire.

Traditionalists are blessed by following set patterns, especially ones handed down by the historical Church, such as repeated liturgies, church calendars, common prayers, structured services, and ancient practices.

Ascetics find deep meaning in denial of common pleasures. The disciplines of meditation, fasting, solitude, chastity, and extended or all-night prayer feed their spirit.

---

19 https://www.focusonthefamily.com/marriage/nine-spiritual-temperaments/. Accessed January 26, 2021.

Activists are replenished through confronting injustices, needs, and challenges—especially on behalf of others.

Caregivers love God by loving others. They get in touch with God's Spirit by touching the lives of others with practical demonstrations of Christ's love.

Enthusiasts are supercharged when worshiping passionately with other believers or when God's supernatural presence and power are emphasized.

Contemplatives are quietly emotional about God. They are filled when they spend time with Jesus, worshiping and enjoying him. They usually love journaling their devotion and experiences.

Which of these grab your heart? You probably have a strong affinity for two, three, or four of these descriptions. It is good to major in those habits. However, you should engage in all nine to mature and deepen your spiritual connection with God.

Following is a list of my favorite and most helpful disciplines described in words meaningful to me and hopefully to you. These practices make my heart "dance" in his presence. They can heal, fill, thrill, and launch us forward with great power.

Silence and solitude: to withdraw from all distractions and to be fully attentive to ourselves and God. These are times we schedule for aloneness, without human or technological interaction, to radically decelerate the pace of life, to "slow the whirl" and simply be in the Spirit's presence. This is a detachment from all that props up our self-image and a gradual immersion of the heart into the stillness of honestly knowing he is God and I am loved.

Creation immersion: to soak in the beauty and joy of nature, knowing "This Is My Father's World" (a traditional hymn worth singing). This is a world where mountains and hills sing (Isaiah 55:12); where skies and heavens pour forth speech and knowledge (Psalm 19); where rivers, fields, and trees clap their hands (Isaiah 55:12; Psalm 98:8); where all creation reveals and testifies to the goodness and love of God.

Fasting and prayer: to deny our flesh something it craves in order to redirect its desires to God himself in prayer. To choose to do "without" so that we might be more "with" the Spirit. To create "thin" places in our own routines where Heaven comes close to our piece of earth. To turn a deaf ear to cries of our desires so that our ear might be more attuned to his still, small voice.

Meditation and contemplation: to mull over in the mind a glorious truth of God's Word, an attribute of the beauty of Jesus, or a glory of God himself. To be lifted above the chaotic rabbit trails of our scattered thoughts and to settle our hearts and minds deeply and peacefully upon the red carpet of his welcoming love that bids us ascend to be with him.

Study and memorization: to engage the research, reasoning, and logic of our mind to mine those deeper truths of his fathomless wisdom. To exercise the mind's energies in the direction of discovery until a tired satisfaction of spiritual fulfillment sweeps over us. To discipline the mind through repetition until a passage is stored safely in the vault of our brain, ready to be accessed at the Spirit's bidding. To grow so familiar with Scripture that it becomes an old friend whose face you delight to see whenever you think on it.

Sacrifice and service: to give freely and cheerfully to the point of discomforting ourselves on behalf of the Kingdom and others. This may be giving time we don't have time to give, energy when we are depleted, or giving money beyond our natural reasoning of financial generosity. Engaging in acts of unrewarded, anonymous service loosens the hold of self-centeredness that clings to us even in our kindest of actions.

Solo and group worship: to express our thoughts and affections to God using our physical bodies whether through shouting, clapping, singing, dancing, playing instruments, kneeling, prostrating ourselves, painting, writing poetry, etc. When we give expression to our adoration, whether individually or with others, we most directly fulfill our created purpose in life. The primary Greek word for worship in the New Testament literally means "to kiss toward." This is an empowering act of intellectually reasonable and emotionally congruent response to who God is and what he has done for us.

Confession to God and trusted others: to allow the Spirit to reveal those attitudes, motives, thoughts, words, and actions that displease God then humbly confess those to God and others we can trust. John Wesley's 22 questions, which the members of his Holy Club asked themselves daily, are a helpful and thorough examination of our lives.[20]

Try asking them of yourself:

1. Am I consciously or unconsciously creating the impression that I am better than I really am? In other words, am I a hypocrite?
2. Am I honest in all my acts and words, or do I exaggerate?
3. Do I confidentially pass on to another what was told to me in confidence?
4. Can I be trusted?
5. Am I a slave to dress, friends, work, or habits?
6. Am I self-conscious, self-pitying, or self-justifying?
7. Did the Bible live in me today?

---

20 https://www.umcdiscipleship.org/resources/everyday-disciples-john-wesleys-22-questions. Accessed January 27, 2021.

8. Do I give it time to speak to me everyday?
9. Am I enjoying prayer?
10. When did I last speak to someone else about my faith?
11. Do I pray about the money I spend?
12. Do I get to bed on time and get up on time?
13. Do I disobey God in anything?
14. Do I insist upon doing something about which my conscience is uneasy?
15. Am I defeated in any part of my life?
16. Am I jealous, impure, critical, irritable, touchy, or distrustful?
17. How do I spend my spare time?
18. Am I proud?
19. Do I thank God that I am not as other people, especially as the Pharisees who despised the publican?
20. Is there anyone whom I fear, dislike, disown, criticize, hold resentment toward, or disregard? If so, what am I doing about it?
21. Do I grumble or complain constantly?
22. Is Christ real to me?

Fellowship and submission: to pursue interactive spiritual relationships with a few other trustworthy believers for the purpose of spiritual growth and service. To submit to the spiritual guidance of those with spiritual insight or spiritual authority over your life. The ability to "spur one another on toward love and good deeds" (Hebrews 10:24-25) and to be "iron sharpening iron" (Proverbs 27:17) is empowering to us.

Rest and celebration: to pause and recline in the assuring power of God's loving care. To demonstrate trust and confidence in God to protect and provide for us, our loved ones, and the work he has called us to. To disengage and receive God's love apart from the work we do for him. Celebration is a form of rest that stops the work to rejoice and "party" in who God is, what he's done, and what he's yet to do.

As we pursue these various habits, we position ourselves for daily empowerment and for an increase in our *capacity* to be empowered. We stretch our spiritual tank. We enlarge our heart volume. We deepen the authenticity of our leadership.

Dallas Willard rightly counsels us about lists such as this one: "But there is no such thing as a complete list of spiritual disciplines, chosen or imposed. Many different activities might be entered into with the aim of finding the manifest grace of God which enables us to do what we cannot do—and be what we cannot be—by direct effort."[21]

Empowerment is to "do what we cannot do—and be what we cannot be—by direct effort," but through our indirect spiritual habits we find ourselves (usually, surprisingly to us) going above and beyond ourselves.

These disciplines often do require a decisive determination. If, however, we find ourselves in drudgery instead of delight regarding them, it is a sign we have degraded them into "works of the flesh" instead of "ways of his grace."

The habits of spiritual empowerment, when done correctly, are always more of a "dance session" than a "gym session." The spiritual disciplines can be a delightful dance that results in greater intimacy and power than you ever thought possible.

---

21 https://dwillard.org/articles/live-life-to-the-full. Accessed January 26, 2021.

CHAPTER 10

The Crew of Empowerment— The Johari Team

Motivational speaker Jim Rohn says, "You are the average of the five people you spend the most time with."[22] While that statement lacks statistical verification, its basic idea is true and biblical.

God tells us to "walk with the wise and become wise, for a companion of fools suffers harm" (Proverbs 13:20). Those we walk with either deflate or elevate our lives. They infuse us or drain us. Your empowerment level will increase (or decrease) as you spend quality time with others.

Compare your spiritual life to a dragon boat. Dragon boat races have become an increasingly popular sport due to the camaraderie and teamwork they require. The crew of a standard dragon boat consists of 22 team members: 20 paddlers in pairs facing toward the bow (front) of the boat, a drummer or caller at the bow, and a steerer standing at the stern (rear) of the boat. The drummer leads the paddlers through the race with a combination of drum beats, voice calls, and hand

---

22   https://www.goodreads.com/quotes/1798-you-are-the-average-of-the-five-people-you-spend

signals. The steerer controls the direction of the boat by positioning a long, straight oar called the steering oar.[23]

Imagine yourself as the steerer. You decide where your boat is heading. The drummer is God's Spirit, calling you forward. The paddlers are those you invite into the boat of your life. These paddlers determine the speed at which your spiritual life advances. They can also influence the direction of the boat by how (and whether) they decide to paddle.

Just because you intend to head quickly in the direction the drummer is calling, it doesn't mean that will necessarily happen. It all depends on your crew, and YOU get to choose them.

There are three types of crew members: rowers, riders, and reversers.

Rowers are those who empower you and power you forward toward the direction the Spirit is calling you. Rowers aren't out to advance themselves or direct the boat in their preferred direction. Rowers are there to serve the steerer and the drummer. They listen to the "drummer" (the Spirit), and they row in sync with his cadence. When the drummer, steerer, and rowers are working together in a unified cadence, the power and progress are dynamic.

Riders are those in your boat who are consuming energy instead of contributing. They aren't rowing; they are riding. They are dead weight.

Some riders may not be paddling because of pain, injury, or exhaustion. If you can carry them for a bit, they may become strong contributors to the speed of your boat. Others may not yet be paddling because they are willing but naive or untaught. If you train them, they may become your strongest teammates.

There are other riders, however, who have little or no interest in helping advance the mission of Christ in their lives or in yours. They aren't

---

[23] https://en.wikipedia.org/wiki/Dragon_boat Accessed December 28, 2020.

there to help you become the leader, the minister, the empowerer God wants you to be. They are enjoying your energy but not adding to it.

"Riders" need to be invested in and observed to see whether they will develop into "rowers." If not, they need to be dropped off and left on the shore of your life, only to be occasionally visited.

Reversers actively resist the mission of your boat. They are paddling in the wrong direction. They may do this deliberately or unconsciously; nevertheless, they are significantly hindering your empowerment level. Whether through bloodline, circumstances, personal history, or poor friend choices, these reversers are people who are on your crew.

Reversers cannot be tolerated. They are working against God's mission and God's call on your life. They won't want to leave your boat, but they must be ordered off. They are people like Alexander the coppersmith, who did great harm to Paul (2 Timothy 4:14). Their negative energy is draining you and hurting the entire crew.

The management of your boat crew is one of the most important tasks of your life. Jesus spent a whole night in prayer before selecting his "boat crew" (Luke 6:12-13). He understood the seriousness of his selections. His team was far from perfect. Yours will be too. But his crew had hearts that were headed in the right direction, as evidenced in their actions after Thomas vowed, "Let us also go, that we may die with him" (John 11:16). They were a "ride or die" crew.

Most pastors and leaders are far too passive in selecting who they want closest to them. They keep people in their boat because of history or compassion or a deception that this is the best they can do. Remember, you as the "steerer" and the Spirit as the "drummer" are the captains of your boat. Don't delegate your skipper's hat.

Your crew is vital to building your Personal Multiplication Capacity.

You need them. You must build a team who will encourage you and exhort you, who will cheer for you but also confront you. God says, "Wounds from a friend can be trusted" (Proverbs 27:6).

Who do you have on your crew, in your circle of five, who can wound you in love so you keep growing toward the dream God has in mind for you? Remember, if you can build God's dream for you by yourself, it's not *God's* dream—it's yours.

One of the most helpful tools for growing into God's dream for your life is the Johari Window.[24] The Johari Window is a tool to give you more self-understanding. It is pictured as a four-paned window into your life.

The upper right pane is the **OPEN SELF** pane. It describes what you know *and* what others know about you.

The lower right pane is the **HIDDEN SELF** pane. It consists of what you know *but* others don't know about you.

The upper left pane is the **BLIND SELF** pane. It includes what you don't know about you *but* others do know about you.

The lower left pane is the **UNKNOWN SELF** pane. It contains what you don't know about you *and* what others don't know about you *but* what God does know about you.

To increase your empowered (y) score, you need a crew or team who will help grow the size of your OPEN SELF window pane. The bigger the OPEN SELF pane, the healthier and more impactful your life will be.

Here's how to use your crew to help you grow:

Share with them more deeply and transparently about your life. This shrinks the HIDDEN SELF pane.

---

24 https://en.wikipedia.org/wiki/Johari_window Accessed October 31, 2023.

Ask them, "What do you see in me that I can't see in myself? What do you hear from others that they see in me that I don't see?" This shrinks the BLIND SELF pane.

Request that they pray *for* you and *with* you, that the Spirit will reveal to you areas of sin or areas of strengths and gifts that you and they cannot see. This diminishes the UNKNOWN SELF pane.

When we develop a few close spiritual friends, we position ourselves to do what we could never do on our own. Even the development of the Johari Window bears this out. Why is it called the Johari Window? Because in 1955 two psychologist friends, Joseph Luft and Harrington Ingham, worked together to create the concept. When they went to name it, they decided to use a combination of their first names, *Joseph* and *Harrington—Johari*.[25]

The right crew can help us allow more and more of God's light to shine through us into the world around us—and we can do the same for them. An empowered, Spirit-led life is not lived independently or individually. It is lived with those who can see the fire on your head and fan it.

---

25 https://en.wikipedia.org/wiki/Johari_window Accessed October 31, 2023.

PART 2
EMPOWERING

CHAPTER 11
Empowering—The Jesus Ministry Method

Your Personal Multiplication Capacity begins and increases with being empowered by the Spirit. The more you are filled with the Spirit, the greater your multiplication potential becomes. But multiplication happens with two factors, two different numbers that interact. When you multiply two numbers, you get a "product" (the math term). What's your product, your PMC?

Can we agree that Jesus had the highest PMC ever? He produced the "product" we must aspire to. How did he do it? How can we do it?

Being **empowered must interact with empowering** *others* **for multiplication to occur.** *Empowered* **leaders must also be** *empowering* **leaders.**

The outflow of being filled with Spirit must be an inflow into the lives of others. The empowered leader must focus that power on empowering their followers. The friend must focus their spiritual vitality on building up their friends. The disciple-maker must zero in on pouring into the disciple for the sake of launching them. The pastor must equip the people for the work of ministry.

We are empowered to spend our lives empowering others.

My ministry story missed this truth. Earlier I described coming as a pastor to our dying urban mono-ethnic church with grandiose ideas about how to grow a big church. Those dreams were for Jesus and for souls but, honestly, they also all led back to me and my leadership.

As we started to implement my vision, the Lord began to do amazing work. We prayer-walked through our multi-ethnic neighborhood praying, "Lord help Light & Life Church look like our neighborhood." We applied church growth principles. We prayed like crazy. What happened? People got saved, believers transferred to our church, small groups got started, ministries began, and we added more and more people to our weekly services. Even though we only had 39 parking spaces, we became the fastest growing church in our denomination.

I was empowered and was gathering lots of people around me. We now had the church size that could help my *real* dream come true: to become a megachurch! But we would have to raise millions of dollars and relocate to a safer area with lots of parking.

As I began to pitch the dream, my wife (who is much more spiritual and empowered than myself) suggested, "Honey, we might want to go away to fast and pray about such a big decision." I couldn't argue with that advice, so we took off on a prayer retreat, and a supernatural thing happened.

As Deb and I were seeking the Lord separately, we were both led to the exact same passage of Scripture, Ezekiel 47:1-12. Through this passage the Lord revealed that we were building a "lake" church, where everyone flowed into one place, around one leader, gave to one budget, helped build one vision, and the goal was to keep everyone in the lake. But God had an Ezekiel 47 vision for us: to be a "river" church, where people flowed in, were equipped and empowered, then they would flow out, to bring the Living Water to other areas by starting churches and ministry. The impact might start as a trickle, a small brook, but over time the multiplication effect would cause us to become a mighty river for Kingdom influence. Verse 9 declares with promise that "where the river flows everything will live."

We were convicted and convinced to pursue a different vision: a vision of empowering and sending disciples into the calling and dreams that God had for their lives. A radical paradigm shift from addition only to multiplication was birthed through that prayer retreat. We began the multiplication journey of being empowered for the purpose of empowering!

Jesus spent his life and ministry empowering his disciples. Approximately 75% of his recorded time in the Gospels was spent with the 12 apostles. But there were times he was with the three: Peter, James, and John. Other times, he was with the 72 disciples. Jesus had different circles of empowerment engagement (as will we), but he was always pouring his life into empowering his closest followers into becoming all God wanted them to be.

I have observed far too many gifted and anointed leaders who were mostly interested in building a bigger platform for themselves to stand on. They enjoyed the spotlight and genuinely believed Jesus was getting the spotlight because they were standing in it with him. In their minds, the bigger their spotlight, the more light would be on Jesus. Their thinking was accurate to a point.

The point where they were deceived was in believing that they were ministering in the most effective way. Addition almost always "feels" better than multiplication. Addition is good up to the point it hinders multiplication. Then it becomes an obstruction to rapid Kingdom advance. This is why every leader must carry a mirror—so when the spotlight hits them, they reflect the light to Jesus and to other developing leaders. Sadly, many leaders absorb the light rather than reflect it.

I had an experience about three years into our new "river" church mission. Although it wasn't at the time, it would later become one of my favorite ministry moments. We were at a public park hosting a picnic as a reunion for several of our recent church plants in the area. I was going around greeting people who had come from the various churches. I introduced myself to a sharp-looking couple who were eating fried chicken with a few others. They were friendly but asked, "Could you say your name again? We haven't ever heard that name before." After I repeated myself more clearly, they said, "No. Haven't heard that name. Are you from one of the Light & Life church plants?" I said, "Yes, I am. I really enjoy the Light & Life family. Have a great day." Ouch to my ego.

Bob Buford, founder of Leadership Network understood this essence of empowering. Probably Bob's most well-known quote was: "My fruit grows on other people's trees." This captures the spirit of Personal Multiplication Capacity. Bob was an empowering leader.

What can I empower that may never have my name on it?

Who can I invest in so that they are empowered to become fruitful for the Kingdom and not just for my ministry?

Who can I invest in that will carry the Kingdom baton so far from me that I may never be known?

These are the Kingdom questions for empowering others.

I am disappointed that my picnic story hasn't happened more in my ministry. I have, sadly, too often made ministry more about me than about other leaders. Our delight must be empowering others above and beyond ourselves—doing this so much and seeing it repeated through them so often that our names are forgotten. To be forgotten by name and only remembered by Jesus—that's a worthy goal.

Well-known leadership researcher and author Jim Collins states that "Level 5 leaders display a powerful mixture of personal humility and indomitable will. They're incredibly ambitious, but their ambition is first and foremost for the cause, for the organization and its purpose, not themselves."[26]

The most impactful leaders are often the least known leaders. This is because they practice empowerment. Instead of consuming, hoarding, or celebrating their power, position, or influence, they distribute it freely to others. We are part of a thriving global organism known as the Church primarily because Jesus was the best empowerer ever. He was the definition of a "Level 5" leader.

Jesus deliberately chose an empowerment model to further his ministry. His ministry plan was not to require people to physically come to him to receive the benefits of the Kingdom. Instead he equipped and empowered his followers to take the Kingdom to where the people were.

Luke 10:1 is an under-utilized passage that explains why Jesus' ministry was so effective: "After this the Lord appointed seventy-two others and sent them two by two ahead of him to every town and place where he was about to go."

---

26 https://www.jimcollins.com/concepts/level-five-leadership.html Accessed January 15, 2022.

This wasn't just Jesus' advance promotional team. Even though Jesus was the central attraction, they weren't just the warm-up act. Jesus delegated genuine power to these 72 disciples: "Heal the sick who are there and tell them, 'The kingdom of God has come near to you'" (Luke 10:9). When they returned they were reporting things like: "Even demons submit to us in your name" (v. 17). Jesus empowered *them* to do what they had been watching *him* do.

Luke 10:2 shares with us what was on Jesus' heart as he sent them: "He told them, 'The harvest is plentiful, but the workers are few. Ask the Lord of the harvest, therefore, to send out workers into his harvest field.'" Jesus' prayer request was tied to his ministry model: more empowered harvesters.

We focus on the 12 disciples but often forget about these 72 unnamed others in addition to the 12. Jesus was first and foremost an equipper of Kingdom workers.

Jesus' focus was never on getting a bigger crowd, but it was always on empowering more workers. You can inspire and motivate crowds, but you can't really empower crowds to multiply the mission. That takes a more personal approach. You see this principle in multi-level sales platforms where success is largely driven by the empowerment of the downline through personal relationships.

Yet, I have asked many groups of pastors across the nation a very simple question about their ministry: Can you name two or three people you are currently discipling? Crickets. An uncomfortable silence comes across the group. Too busy writing a sermon (something Jesus *never* modeled or commanded) to make disciples (something Jesus *constantly* modeled and commanded).

Read the Gospels and you will find Jesus' priority on the

transmission of power through relationship. This is the place where the Church has missed the discipleship boat. Christian celebrities are those who stand in the spotlight, speak to thousands, build large auditoriums, have the most followers on social media, dress the coolest, wear the expensive sneakers, and write the bestsellers. But those who follow Jesus' method of empowerment are often the unknown.

This is the friction point. To follow Jesus' way of empowerment requires nailing our ego to the cross daily and handing off power in every way we can.

Jesus is speaking of his death and burial in John 12:24 when he says, "Very truly I tell you, unless a kernel of wheat falls to the ground and dies, it remains only a single seed. But if it dies, it produces many seeds." But he was also describing his model of ministry! Seeds have to become unseen as they go into the dirt of their mission. They have to die to their desire to be seen and celebrated. It is in that place of surrender that empowerment of others is possible. If this process doesn't happen, the seed might be huge, but it will be lonely.

The *coco de mer* tree, also known as "the sea coconut," has the largest seed on earth. It can be as large as 50 pounds (really difficult to plant in your backyard)! But as impressive as this seed is, unless it germinates, it will be a solo seed. Instead of a multiplier of other trees, it will be a big seed that slowly begins to rot. Jesus' small kernel of wheat that dies in order to multiply significantly out-produces the huge sea coconut seed that fails to die. Whether to be a "big seed" or to produce "many seeds" is really a daily decision for the disciple.

I remember attending the fifth anniversary service of one of our church plants. I had invested in the planter who had raised up other leaders who were now leading the church. It was a church plant that our church had given many key families to. As the service went on, I began to think, "They aren't even going to introduce me or acknowledge me. How rude; how ungrateful; how negligent!"

Suddenly the Holy Spirit showed up with his scalpel to do some heart surgery. I sensed the Spirit probing, "Larry, did you plant the church for your glory or mine? Are you rejoicing over what I am doing here or pouting over not getting some of the credit? Are you only going to empower people and ministries that will retain some of your name?" I was convicted that the "seed" of my life needed to die a deeper death to multiply more life.

Your leadership quest is not to lead more people but to empower more people to lead. This is the difference between centralizing power and decentralizing power. You want to invest your power to release the gifts, potential, strengths, anointing, and brilliance you see in others.

An essential key to empowering others as Jesus did is to understand the relationship between the triad of *why*, *how*, and *what*.

The influential book *Start with Why—How Great Leaders Inspire Others to Take Action* by Simon Sinek has explained the Empowerment Factor from a secular standpoint with surprising clarity. His thesis is simple: Most companies start with "what"—What are we building, offering, selling?; they move to "how"—How are we going to build it, offer it, sell it?; and they often never really arrive at "why"—Why are we doing this in the first place? However, he writes that the profoundly influential and successful companies (think Apple, Harley Davidson, Southwest Airlines) almost always prioritize starting from and focusing on their "why."

I have often thought of Simon Sinek's work as being a distillation of Jesus' empowerment model. Jesus, through Paul, would teach us that until we get to Heaven the three empowering attitudes are "faith, hope, and love. But the greatest of these is love" (1 Corinthians 13:13).

Paul powerfully brings this triad together in 1 Thessalonians 1:3: "We remember before our God and Father your work produced by faith, your labor prompted by love, and your endurance inspired by hope in our Lord Jesus Christ."

Jesus' empowerment model aligns the "why" of love with the "what" of hope and the "how" of faith. Love is the motive. Hope is the mission. Faith is the method.

LOVE is the "why" of everything in God's Kingdom.

Love is the MOTIVE.

God's love sent and gave his Son (John 3:16).

We love him because he first loved us (1 John 4:19).

The greatest commandment is to love God and our neighbor (Matthew 22:36-40).

The new commandment of Jesus is to love one another as Christ has loved us (John 13:34).

Paul declared, "Christ's love compels us" (2 Corinthians 5:14).

If we don't have love, then our "what" and our "how" are just noisy gongs (1 Corinthians 13).

Jesus loved his disciples as friends, taught them how to receive the love of his Father, demonstrated how to love others, and passed his mission of love onto them. Jesus started with the "why" of love as the motivation for everything he and his disciples would do.

HOPE is the vision of "what" we desire to see happen: multiplicative disciple-making.

Hope is the MISSION.

Hope pictures a preferred future.

Hope commits itself to a specific direction to channel the motivation of our "why."

Hope states what we want our lives, our families, our churches, our followers to produce.

Jesus' "what" was clear from beginning to end.

His first call was, "Follow me ... and I will send you out to fish for people" (Matthew 4:19).

His last commission was, "Go and make disciples" (Matthew 28:19).

Every follower of Jesus should be crystal clear on the "what" of our mission.

FAITH is "how" we believe it will happen.

Faith is the METHOD.

Faith is the connection between our motive and our mission.

Hope says WHAT we want to happen.

Love states WHY we want to happen.

Faith joins our love to our hope by declaring, "I believe it will happen, and I will do what the Spirit leads me to do to help *make* it happen!"

Empowering others requires an unwavering faith that God is at work through you and that he wants to use you in someone else's life—not because you're "good enough," "know enough," or "pray enough," but because you are available to the Spirit and focused on someone else's empowerment.

Empowering others also demands a faith that God is at work in your followers/disciples. You believe in them because you believe in the Spirit's work in them. Your faith in them is tangible, and it helps them to deepen their trust in God and believe more in themselves. Faith creates a loving relationship between you and someone else. It seeks to help them obey Jesus and reach for all God has for their lives.

We must always start with the motivation of love, a clear vision of hope, and the unwavering commitment of faith in action to empower others into the dreams God has for their lives. No matter who God places in your path to empower, you must: 1) LOVE them authentically, which is *why* you want to empower them; 2) HOPE God's best for them, which is *what* you are praying for and working toward; and 3) have FAITH in *how* God will use you and will work in them.

Jesus' method of reaching the world with the gospel was not to reach as many as he could during this lifetime. It was to deeply empower a few who would reach the many.

How do we strategically empower other believers so they will rise up to the call of multiplication for the sake of the Kingdom? I believe circles and questions can greatly help us in this quest. Read on!

CHAPTER 12

Empowering Your Circles of Influence—Playing Favorites

The well-known anthropologist Robin Dunbar has done extensive research and concluded that most people can have 5 intimate bonds of friendship, 15 close friends, 50 friends, and 150 casual friends.[27]

Whether these specific numbers are accurate can be debated, but what can't be argued is that people have a variety of concentric circles of relationships. For the sake of our discussion on empowerment, we'll call these "circles of influence."

Everyone has circles of influence. Do you know yours?

If we are seeking to raise our empowering level on the x scale, we must think "multimodal." This means we live each day asking, "Who can I empower today, and how?"

The "who" encompasses a range of relationships from the high-school student at the counter of McDonald's to your spouse and children to the staff member you are preparing to lead the church.

---

27 https://www.goodtherapy.org/blog/psychology-facts/how-many-friends-does-average-person-have-0208197. Accessed October 29, 2023.

When we begin to have a multiplication mindset manifested by an "empowered to empower others" attitude, we move through our day differently. From spontaneous moments of brief encounters to strategic sessions with formally identified disciples, we are seeking to give away the blessing, the anointing, the wisdom, the truth, the zeal, the love, the life that we are receiving from the Spirit. As we live with the flame on our own head (Acts 2:3), we are seeking to pass on the fire on to others.

The "how" includes a variety of modes (multimodal) depending on the proximity of the person we are engaging with. Proximity means what circle they are in, within my circles of influences. The tools of impact that you use will be different for a stranger you are sitting next to at a basketball game than for one of your children or for a staff member you are coaching about their ministry.

To be effective and healthy in empowerment you must identify your circles of influence and who is in what circle. You cannot and should not try to invest at the same level in all your relationships.

Our circles of influence fall into concentric circles with a small inner circle, four or five middle circles, and a larger outer circle.

As you study the life of Jesus, you quickly find that he had favorites. (Yes, Jesus played favorites.) He loved all equally but invested in his followers unequally. His circles can possibly be identified as falling into six or seven levels. His empowering of people helps us think in circles of 3, 12, 24, 72, 120, and 500.

There were the 3 (Peter, James, and John) who were his inner circle. His greatest investment was in these three, who would be the leaders of leaders.

Then the other 12 disciples were his second circle. Jesus would bring these 12 close enough to see the glories and the heartbreaks of ministry. The next circle is an unidentified number that I hypothetically label as "the 24." This was made up of those who most often traveled with him, the 12 disciples plus the women who traveled with him. Luke 8:1-3 names three of those women then states that "many other women" were in that travel group; so let's just call it 12 women disciples.

A fourth circle of Jesus would be the 72 anonymous disciples who were sent out by Jesus in Luke 10:1. They must have spent some time training with Jesus.

A fifth circle might be the 120 who gathered in the upper room to wait for the promise of the Father in Acts 1:15. These probably included most of the 72, but about 50 others had followed closely enough to risk their lives by meeting together in Jerusalem following the crucifixion.

A sixth circle could be composed of the 500 brothers and sisters Jesus chose to manifest himself to after his resurrection (1 Corinthians 15:6). What an empowering encounter Jesus had with this vast circle of followers!

A seventh circle could simply be labeled "the crowd" that included as many as 5,000 or more who gathered to hear his teaching or eat his miraculous bread and fish.

These neatly packaged circles do not, however, accurately represent everyone Jesus invested in. For example, Lazarus might fit into one of Jesus' more inner circles. Where might Nicodemus fit? Or what empowering influence did Jesus have on his cousin, John the Baptist?

The point is not to clearly label people in Jesus' ministry nor in our ministry lives. The idea is to free us to invest differently and strategically in various levels of relationships. To raise our empowering level, we must be thinking, "Who should I be investing in, to what degree, and how can I most effectively empower them?"

Who are your 3, 12, 24, 72, 120, or 500? Are you asking the Lord about who fits where in your circles of influence? Whoever these people are, many of them will change over time. We must make the stewardship of who we are empowering an ongoing matter of prayer.

Another question is what *type of relationship* will you have with those in the different circles? Will they be your disciples, your students, your mentees, or your audience? Will you be a disciple-maker, a coach, a mentor, or a teacher to them? What's the difference between these roles anyway?

While there are a variety of definitions for these terms, it's helpful to be able to distinguish for yourself what type of investment you are going to make in the individuals around you. While a thorough dissection and description of these terms may be beneficial, what really matters is what the terms mean to *you*. Here's how I use them:

Discipling is walking with a person to help them obey all that Jesus has commanded us as they draw more and more fully on his presence and power. Discipleship is helping a person become more like Jesus by offering yourself as a model. It echoes what Paul said in 1 Corinthians 11:1, "Follow my example, as I follow the example of Christ." It is holistic, intending to impact the totality of the disciple's life. Although teaching certain skills may be a *part* of discipling, it is focused on attitudes, actions, reasoning, values, character, words, etc. Discipleship has a two-fold goal: 1) to be more and more like Christ, and 2) to become a disciple-maker of others.

Direct discipleship requires close proximity. Disciples are not made in a classroom but in the rough and tumble realities of life—in the mundane moments, in the disappointments, in the victories, in the temptations, in the ins and outs of living out faith on a daily basis.

There is a powerful discipleship word that is used only once in Scripture, but it brilliantly captures so much of Jesus' empowerment of his disciples. John 3:22 says that "after this, Jesus and his disciples went out into the Judean countryside, where he spent some time with them, and baptized." The Greek word translated "spent some time with them" is *diatribo*.

Diatribo literally means "to rub in." In New Testament times, *diatribo* was used to describe breaking in a pair of sandals. The goal was for the sandals to conform to the individual's feet so that they would serve the owner well. The sandals were to take the owner wherever they needed to go. But the only way for sandals to be broken in was for the owner to walk with them. The more they walked together, the more the sandals would take on the unique shape of the master's feet.

Jesus "rubbed himself into" his disciples by spending time with them, letting his Word and character shape them into who he was. For our 3 or our 12 (and maybe even our 24) we must get close enough so we "rub off" on them and help them conform to Jesus.

Perhaps the most powerful teaching I have ever given on prayer happened in the dusty hills above Oakland. I was spending a whole day with the two men I was discipling. We were on a seven-mile hike, and I decided I wanted to teach on prayer. So I told them, "Let me share with you how I pray the Lord's Prayer." Then for the next 30 minutes as we hiked, I prayed through the Lord's Prayer, expanding each phrase to capture how it related to my life and theirs. I didn't expound, I just prayed. A few weeks later, one of my disciples said, "I am walking every day and spending an hour praying the Lord's Prayer, and it's so powerful for me!" *Diatribo* in action.

Coaching (for me) is drawing out of a person what God has put into them. Helping them discover their gifts, their talents, their personality traits, and moving them toward defined goals. Coaching is me telling them where they need to improve in their lives. This demands less relationship than discipling but more relationship than mentoring.

Mentoring is closely related to coaching, and perhaps we are straining to delineate any difference. But (for me) mentoring is imparting what God has put into me into someone else. Mentoring is focused more on developing certain skills in my mentee. I can mentor in certain areas of life. For example I mentor in areas such as marriage, preaching, leadership, board management, writing, parenting, and church planting.

Teaching is imparting knowledge that will be transformative, inspiring, and solidifying—sharing Kingdom principles that the student or listener must then take and apply to their lives and situations. There is little relationship necessary.

If we are pursuing a higher Personal Multiplication Capacity, to be more empowered and to be empowering to more people, then we will begin to collect stories of impact from the various circles around our lives.

Our inner circles are where we will have the greatest impact, but we may be surprised to find that we have significant influence on some in our outer circles. These are the stories you probably won't hear until Heaven. But once in a while God will give you an affirming glimpse of the impact you may be having.

Recently, I was at a conference of 2,000 pastors and leaders. After one of the services, folks were encouraged to come forward and spend an hour or two in prayer. I was kneeling down in front for about half an hour when a woman tapped me on the shoulder. I turned around and saw a middle-aged woman smiling at me with tears in her eyes, and she asked, "Do you remember me?" I weakly replied, "I think so." Then she stated with great emotion, "You are my spiritual father! I was in your church for a while about 20 years ago, and then we moved out of state. Your words burned in my heart, and I went into ministry and am serving the Lord because of your influence."

When you seek to live on fire and light fires in others, you never know where the Spirit will take the flame.

EMPOWERING QUESTIONS: What Our Disciples and Followers Really Want to Know

Much of our empowering of others will take place through small deposits in the outer circles of our influence. Our most significant and influential investments, however, will be with those in our 3, 12, or 24 circles. This is the depth of relationship necessary for a person to be significantly shaped by your life and friendship.

This is why Howard Hendricks, powerful professor and author, adamantly contended, "If you cannot be accused of exclusivity, you are not discipling."[28] If you are trying to help everyone equally, you will bless everyone and disciple no one. You must focus on your inner circles of influence.

Hendricks also sagely taught that "we teach what we know, but we reproduce who we are."[29] You can teach a large group, but you must model your teaching if you want to truly empower. For this to happen, you must let people see who you really are, not just what you know.

Great leaders understand this. Adam Morris is the President of Azusa

---

28 https://www.willmancini.com/blog/epic-quotes-on-discipleship-influence-from-prof-howard-hendricks-1924-2013
29 https://www.willmancini.com/blog/epic-quotes-on-discipleship-influence-from-prof-howard-hendricks-1924-2013

Pacific University, one of the largest evangelical Universities in America. Dr. Morris is incredibly busy, but he believes he is called to make disciples, not just to lead an institution. So he leads a discipleship group of students weekly. Not only is he having a life-changing influence on a few students, but his example is shaping the university culture and setting the standard for his 1,200 staff and faculty.

As we engage in these deeper relationships with the intent of reproducing our life of faith and zeal in a handful of individuals, we discover that there are some common questions our disciples/mentees/followers are asking. We need to know these questions and answer them effectively to help those we are empowering reach their full potential.

I have identified seven "Big Questions" we need to answer for our disciples, mentees, or students. Chapters 13-19 take an in-depth look at each question and impact on those we are seeking to empower. As you answer these questions more authentically, effectively, and thoroughly, your empowering score will begin to soar.

CHAPTER 13
The Empowering Connection— The Question of Love

Fumi Chito is a fruitful pastor in Japan, but he probably would not be if Ralph Moore had not valued him. Fumi Chito's pivot point came when Ralph was the keynote speaker for a pastor's conference on disciple-making at Hope Chapel's largest church plant in Japan.

Fumi was not a pastor leading anything in the church, and therefore he could not attend. There were stringent cultural rules that separated him from the pastors. The room was full to capacity, with standing room only, which precluded anyone other than leaders from attending. But Fumi had a passion for Jesus and his mission. So Fumi would sit outside the door in the cold of winter to hear Ralph. He listened by leaning against the door while sitting on three pillows, wrapped in a heavy jacket and a blanket for warmth.

After a time, Ralph saw Fumi sitting outside and asked him to come in. Fumi declined. The pastors explained to Ralph that Fumi was not invited. But Ralph saw a heart in Fumi that he was determined to nurture. He insisted that Fumi come in, otherwise he would not continue. The pastors relented, and Fumi became a personal disciple of Ralph's. Following this example, other pastors decided to disciple Fumi, who became the primary worship leader in the rapidly growing church. From there he planted Crossroad Church in Nishinomiya, Japan. The church has multiplied four times since.

Fumi has gone on to be a leader of leaders in Japan. I sat at a table eating Texas BBQ with some of the best-known leaders in the American Church, and Fumi was sitting there right beside Ralph. He wasn't out in the cold any longer.

Do you think Ralph is an empowering leader who has a high Personal Multiplication Capacity? Absolutely. Individuals feel valued and loved by Ralph. Ralph isn't looking to hang out with the big names or find the next superstar. Ralph is looking for the next Fumi to connect with and empower into multiplication.

Empowering others begins with communicating authentic love. Too many leaders are trying to teach multiplication to an individual's mind. You might be able to "add" that way, but you can't multiply. You first teach multiplication to a person's heart.

Paul wrote to his friends in Thessalonica, "Because we loved you so much, we were delighted to share with you not only the gospel of God but our lives as well" (1 Thessalonians 2:8). The message was not just the words of the gospel but the love of Paul, which he demonstrated through sharing his life with them.

The Thessalonians became eager to share the message Paul brought because they experienced the love that Paul shared with them. Love creates the bridge that connects our message *to* someone with the mission that God has *for* someone.

Every follower wants to know, "Do they love me? Do they value me?

Do they want the best for me?" For our impact to truly stick in the lives of those we disciple, mentor, or lead, they must feel valued and loved. They must be convinced that we are not trying to use them to further our own agenda or notoriety. Such uncertainty about a leader's motives will undermine the empowerment process. Followers must sincerely believe that their leader is a "hero maker," using their platform to promote others instead of themselves.

My friend Dave Ferguson, pastor of Community Christian Church, CEO of Exponential, and Lead Visionary for New Thing, has literally written the book on heromaking. Dave's emphasis on developing people into the mission God has for them has been demonstrated over decades. Dave is out to make heroes out of those close to him, and they feel the love. It's why he and his leaders have placed an emphasis on training apprentices at every level of ministry. If you are a leader who serves with Dave, your main ministry task is not the ministry itself but finding and empowering an apprentice to replace you and making a hero of them. This approach is so pervasive that Dave currently has a lead pastor apprentice who will take the reins of the church in the future.

Can you imagine how important the disciples must have felt when they saw more than 5,000 people on a crowded hillside hanging on Jesus' every word? Then they saw Jesus feed them all. Then Jesus turned to the disciples and said, "Hey, guys I want to hang out with just the 12 of you for a while. Let's go to the other side of the lake" (Mark 6:30-46).

Jesus could *teach* the 5,000, but he couldn't *disciple* them into being multipliers. He could *love* the 5,000, but he couldn't be close enough to *demonstrate* the depth and power of that personal love. For that, he chose 12 men who would multiply into a movement.

How empowering was it for Jesus to say, "Listen, guys, you aren't servants. You are my friends" (John 15:15)? Then to deepen the value statement and basically say, "I chose you because I saw the potential in you. You are going to go do great things!" (v. 16). How are you conveying this sense of importance to your circle of influence? Do they feel like friends? Do they sense the great value you see in them? Do they know they are loved for who they are, not for what they can do?

I recall hearing the powerful Kenyan pastor Bishop Oscar Muriu say, "I don't send out church planters. I send out sons and daughters." His connection of love is so real that it is like sending his own blood sons and daughters off to war.

Many church leaders want to lead from the invulnerability of the pulpit, or the coolness of the podium, or the distance of their teaching gift, or the security of the group setting. Most pastors have been hurt when they let their love go too deep with individual disciples. So they retreat to the safety of protected kindness instead of forging forward to the power of contagious vulnerability.

Empowering means living at the cross, where your heart can be both pierced and healed, where you can be the wounded and the healer at the same time. If you love deeply you will almost certainly be hurt deeply, but you will also empower more fully.

It is this determination to value your disciples and demonstrate that value through sharing your life that unleashes the Empowerment Factor. Your followers feel your love and become ready to learn, grow, serve, and adventure with you into new and challenging ministry territory. Here are some tools to help you.

5 EMPOWERING PRACTICES TO COMMUNICATE PERSONAL LOVE

1. Say it privately. Frequently and clearly articulate your heart: "I really value you." "I love you, my friend." "Our friendship is so valuable to me." "I am so blessed to have you in my life." "I see you as my son or daughter in the faith."

2. Say it publically. Speak well of them in front of others, especially when they are around to hear it. "Sean is really a treasured ministry partner and friend." "Joel is one of the most devoted Christ-followers I know." "I have learned so much from being with Paul."

3. Keep exploring. Continue to discover their story, both past and present. The details of their lives are important. Who has influenced them? What events have shaped them? How are they feeling today? What's on their heart? What are the greatest desires and deepest fears?

4. Extend their value. Get to know their families, friends, hobbies, interests, etc. Who and what is important to them at this stage of their lives? What do they love doing? People feel valued when you value what they value.

5. Conduct an analysis. Inquire about their fears, dreams, challenges, doubts, and aspirations. Share your own and ask about theirs. Prayerfully analyze the present together, and then seek to address it with discernment, wisdom, and prayer.

John, the beloved disciple, writes this amazing sentence about how deeply Jesus loved those he was dining with in the upper room on the eve of his crucifixion: "Jesus knew that the hour had come for him to leave this world and go to the Father. Having loved his own who were in the world, he loved them to the end" (John 13:1).

Through the good times and bad, through their faith and their doubts, through their victories and failures, Jesus loved them all the way to his ministry finish line. His love is what made for such a successful baton handoff on the day of Pentecost. His empowered disciples were ready to risk their lives for the mission of the One who had loved them "to the end." Does your love impact your disciples in the same way?

CHAPTER 14

The Empowering Cause—The Question of Mission

I slowly looked around the table and saw seven eager and earnest faces. Different ethnicities, various ages, a variety of gifts, very divergent life stories—yet deeply united by Jesus' grace and mission.

These guys were not professional ministers. They were not ordained. They weren't drawing ministry paychecks. Almost all of them were "unschooled, ordinary" men (Acts 4:13). Membership in this group was by invitation only. The bar for entry was high. The first criteria: "You can be in this group if you are willing to do anything Jesus wants you to do and go anywhere he wants you to go!" I called it the "MOG" group, which stood for "Ministers of God," and the guys called each other "MOGS."

These were men hungry to take the ball and run with it. Their only questions were: "Where's the goal line, Coach?" "What is going to put points on Heaven's scoreboard?" "What does our mission together and individually look like?"

Every follower wants to know, "Where are we going?" The MOGS were willing to lay their lives down for Jesus, but they needed more direction in order to turn their zeal into an organized mission. So we laid a map of our city of 500,000 out on the table. I pointed out the nine city council districts and highlighted something specific about each of them. Then I said, "I believe we should try and start a new Light & Life Church in the other eight city council districts! Who is willing to lay down their lives for this city by helping start new district-focused churches?" They were all in, and Mission 2010 was born! Their passion had been hot, but now it went to boiling.

At 211 degrees, water is hot. At 212 degrees, it boils. Hot water is good and useful for many things. But boiling water is powerful. Boiling water creates steam. Steam is potent enough to move a 500-ton locomotive pulling thousands of tons of freight.

Often the one-degree difference is a simple, clearly defined goal that captures the imagination and inspires passionate action. Embracing a cause or a mission on a deep personal level propels a person into sacrificial behaviors that create impact.

As Dr. Martin Luther King Jr. so powerfully declared, "I submit to you that if a man hasn't discovered something he will die for, he isn't fit to live."[30] Dr. King was telling us that only a worthy life mission can draw out of a person a power and passion for living. Empowering leaders help others light the fire of personal mission.

Jesus was the most empowering leader to ever live. When he called out his disciples he did so with these words: "Come, follow me … and I will send you out to fish for people" (Matthew 4:19).

The first two Big Questions of empowerment are invoked in this

---

30 http://www.quotationspage.com/quote/24968.html Accessed September 5, 2021.

simple invitation: "Come, follow me" is a declaration of value and *love*, an invitation to relationship. "Send you out to fish for people" is a definition of *mission*, an invitation to an individual purpose. Jesus was essentially saying, "You have been fishing for fish, going through the motions of life. I will teach you and send you to fish for people, living for a mission in life." Empowering leaders help followers imagine God's dream for their lives.

I asked the seven MOGS seated at a round table, "Can you see yourself as a pastor or key leader in one of these eight new churches in our city? Do you hear God calling to you personally?" I wanted to turn the *idea* of mission into an *individualization* of mission. I wanted to stir their imaginations and move "mission vision" to "mirror vision." Mirror vision is when you look yourself straight in the eyes and say, "By God's grace and call, I can see myself in this mission. I will give my life for a season or a lifetime to further this particular mission."

The imagination is a potent gift God has given to empower us. When our imagination is submitted to God then stirred by the Spirit to picture a preferred future for ourselves and others, great energy builds toward a mission. Mirror vision propels the determination to see imagination lead to creation.

Most pastors err on one side or the other of mission/vision. Many pastors make their own vision too consuming. This means that every individual in the church is there to build the pastor's vision. While this approach helps individual believers escape the hard work of receiving a personal ministry vision and may help them find a significant place of volunteering, it fails to stir their imaginations and passion. It also fails to release the full variety of mission God has purposed for his church. This is a "We can build it; you can help" approach.

On the other side are the many pastors who have no clear vision for their church. Church members aren't stirred to imagine "God-dreams" for their church or their lives. Members are called on to volunteer to keep the church machine running, but individual mission callings are ignored.

The sweet spot of empowering comes when believers are treated as part of a "royal priesthood" of "everyday missionaries." Each has a unique design and call from God to live on their specific mission, and those individual visions are at some level connected with the body of Christ, the Church, to work together to build up the Kingdom of God. When the Church exists to empower the mission of individual believers and to connect them for the greater Jesus mission, then incredible Kingdom works begin to happen. This is an empowering, "You can build it; we can help!" approach.

An essential part of empowering others to mission is the incarnational transmission of mission. Mission is not a theoretical subject, a strategy in a notebook or slide deck, or even a spiritual pep rally with intense prayer over the map of a city. You empower mission in others when you are putting in the actual work, and then you ask them to get their hands dirty with you—when you are living it and not just posting about it.

As I stood in that circle of MOGS with our hands placed on the map of our city, I knew I had to lead by example. I knew the Spirit was calling me to give up my Sunday afternoons and evenings to help plant the first church of Mission 2010. Consequently, my wife (Deb), our teenage daughter (Lindsey), and I started gathering neighbors and friends in our home in City Council District 3. Soon we were holding services on Sunday evenings in the local community center, and a church was born. As I *modeled* the mission, the MOGS *caught* the mission.

One of the seven MOGS, Jim Blythe, was a high-powered COO of a successful company. His heart became so stirred for the mission that he quit his lucrative job to plant a church in one of the city council districts of Long Beach.

One of Jim's favorite sayings was "Burn the ships!" It referred to the oft-told (somewhat erroneous) story of the Spanish explorer Cortez landing at present-day Vera Cruz, Mexico, and then burning the ships so no retreat would be possible. It was a "do or die trying" mindset. For Jim, the mission was so compelling that he was willing to do whatever it took to build the church in District 8 of Long Beach. Jim and Karin Blythe birthed a fruitful church, and the Kingdom has advanced because of their commitment.

5 EMPOWERING PRACTICES TO EMBRACE MISSION

1. Discover their calling. Help followers deeply understand and embrace both their general and unique calling from God. Their general call is clear from Scripture "to make disciples who make disciples." Their unique call is the Ephesians 2:10 calling "to do good works, which God prepared in advance for us to do." (See the book *MORE— Find Your Personal Calling and Live Life to the Fullest Measure* by Todd Wilson.)

2. Surrender. Prayerfully help followers discern what obstacles, idols, sins, or lies may be hindering their full surrender to God's mission. When Jesus was defining the cost of discipleship he used these challenging words of invitation: "Whoever wants to be my disciple must deny themselves and take up their cross daily and follow me" (Luke 9:23).

3. Set a vision. Help disciples seek the Spirit to help them imagine different scenarios that God may want to bring into reality as they go on mission with Jesus. The Lord may give a literal vision, but it is more often a sanctified and submitted imagination of what it would look like to be powerfully used by God. These imaginations are like seeing the building before drawing the blueprints or digging the foundation. Praying in faith in the direction of that internalized vision is empowering.

4. Get honest. Talk honestly about the pains and joys of being on mission with Jesus. We want disciples to embrace the reality of the mission, not just the romance of it. Most leaders either fail to be honest about the sacrifice, or they fail to celebrate small and large victories loudly enough.

5. Tell stories. Tell stories and have others tell stories of the mission. Stories of others quicken the imaginations of those accepting the mission. Empowering leaders are collectors of "God stories," stories of the Spirit working in little and large ways through ordinary people on mission with Jesus.

All seven of those MOGS (and others who followed them) went on to be church planting pastors or key leaders in new churches. They became enthralled with Jesus and his mission. They saw themselves as being vital to the mission, and that vision empowered them into action.

Empowering leaders excel in helping followers see God's vision for their lives and get on mission with him. This is key to building your Personal Multiplication Capacity. How well are you doing?

CHAPTER 15

The Empowering Key—The Question of Trust

I was 17, and I wasn't sure, but I thought I might want to study to be a pastor when I went to college. I was uncertain, so I signed up for a high school class that gave me three hours every afternoon to apprentice in the field of my choice. Harold (who I have written about earlier), the pastor of our small Kansas church, took me under his wing.

He started me off as a janitor. I spent the afternoons cleaning toilets and dusting pews, except when we would have our afternoon talks and prayer time. After three weeks, Harold said, "Larry, you know the church is not the building; it's the people. But the church building is a sacred space, and only four people have the keys to this building. But I am going to trust you with a set of keys. You can come in to work or worship or bring people here whenever you want."

Harold's words and action of trust empowered me in ways that impacted the trajectory of my life. That is the power of trust. His trust gave me something to live up to and a confidence to try new and bigger things with my life. Empowering leaders look for ways to communicate trust.

Every follower wants to know, "How much does my leader trust me?" Trust is the glue between leader and follower, the pipeline between teacher and student. Trust is the catapult that launches disciples forward into God's future for them. *Trusting* empowers *trying*. When followers feel trusted, they are willing to try what is new or difficult.

Jesus empowered his disciples through trust. The gospel mission was going to be entrusted to them. They were God's Plan A, and there was no Plan B. Knowing this, Jesus began to entrust them with Kingdom truth and power early on in their relationship. Soon he was handing them the "keys of the kingdom" (Matthew 16:19).

Peter in particular received these "keys." We almost chuckle at this because of Peter's propensity to "miss the point" and confuse zeal with wisdom. Just four verses after giving Peter the "keys," Jesus is looking at Peter and saying, "Get behind me, Satan" (Matthew 16:23). It makes me want to ask with incredulity, "And you're letting *Peter* drive the Kingdom bus?" But Jesus knows what he's doing. In fact, he teaches that to whom much is entrusted, much will be asked (Luke 12:48). If you expect a lot, you must trust a lot.

Peter ends up taking those keys and opening the doors for people to come into the Kingdom. In Acts 2, Peter preaches the message, and 3,000 Jews are saved. In Acts 8, Peter and John show up, and the Samaritans receive the Holy Spirit. In Acts 10, Peter unlocks the door for the Gentiles to come into the Kingdom. Jesus trusted an imperfect, immature, but big-hearted disciple with the keys. That trust empowered Peter to do significant Kingdom ministry.

Trust is not closing our eyes, putting fingers in our ears, crossing our fingers, then wishing for the best. The phrase "Trust but verify" was made famous by Ronald Reagan in December 1987 after the signing of the INF Treaty with Mikhail Gorbachev. The Russian leader quipped, "You repeat that at every meeting," to which Reagan replied, "I like it."[31]

We have all experienced the pain of trusting too much or too soon. But what most leaders miss is the negative consequences of trusting too little or too late. Jesus lived in the balance. Consider the fact that Jesus had spent hundreds of hours in hundreds of circumstances with Peter before he handed him the keys. Peter still kept blowing it, but Jesus handed him the keys anyway.

You see, Jesus' trust was not based on Peter's spiritual understanding but upon Peter's heart and the Holy Spirit's help. Jesus had watched Peter's heart and faith in action. He knew Peter's desires and commitment. But more important, Jesus was looking ahead to who Peter would be once he was filled with the Holy Spirit. Jesus promised that the Spirit would lead and guide Peter into all truth (John 14:26). And that's exactly what happened.

Too often leaders fail to exercise the trust necessary to launch their followers into action. They fear their disciples will fail, and it will damage them. They fear their disciples might hurt someone by misusing the sword (like Peter did). They fear their followers may make them look bad as a leader.

There is a risk aversion that causes leaders to withhold trust for too long. The result is fewer failures but many more "failures to launch." It's "Ready, aim, aim, aim, aim … lost the fire!" This risk aversion is the greater failure.

Wharton School at the University of Pennsylvania did a study that

---

31 https://leadergrow.com/articles/trust-but-verify/ Accessed September 26, 2023.

analyzed over 2.5 million putts from the top 20 golfers on the PGA tour. They found that "fear of a bogey" (taking one more shot than par) prompted golfers to putt safely rather than to take a riskier shot. The fear of the bogey was greater than the thrill of the birdie (taking one one less shot than par). This risk aversion resulted in an average one-stroke loss per 72-hole tournament, with a combined annual loss of $1.2 million in potential prize money.[32]

We need more disciplers and leaders who "take the shot," people who are playing to win, not "to not lose." I have been criticized by leaders who feel that I launch new pastors too early. They may be right, and I am working to better prepare our church planting pastors. However, those who are my biggest critics have failed to launch *any* leaders. They are playing it safe, keeping the Kingdom doctrinally pure in non-essential details as their Kingdom impact shrinks dramatically. Blind trust is foolish. Calculated, Spirit-informed trust is risky—but it's also powerful!

One of the young men (to remain unnamed) I have mentored into the pastorate is Peter's twin brother. His zeal and mouth have put him in the proverbial "doghouse" more times than I can count. A few folks left the church as I empowered him more. He's failed me a few times. I, however, trust his heart. I have watched his ministry actions. (Trust, but verify.) But even much more I trust the Holy Spirit, who has a firm grip on his life and the Spirit.

The day I handed him the keys to the church was a headline day in his life. A kid who used to 'break and enter" was being handed the keys

---

[32] David G Pope and Maurice E. Schweitzer, *Is Tiger Woods Loss Averse? Persistent Bias in the Face of Experience, Competition, and High Stakes* (2007), https://knowledge.wharton.upenn.edu/article/avoiding-the-agony-of-a-bogey-loss-aversion-in-golf-and-business Accessed September 29, 2021.

to help people enter the house of God. That display of trust was one of the most empowering events in his life thus far. He has used those keys to introduce many to Christ, to mentor many disciples, and to enter vocational pastoral ministry. I often think, "What if I hadn't exercised trust?"

6 EMPOWERING PRACTICES TO DEVELOP TRUST

1. Be trustworthy. Model that you can be trusted. Keep your word. Apologize when you fail. Demonstrate impeccable integrity. Keep a promise even when it demands sacrifice. Don't overpromise and underdeliver.

2. Be progressive. Find ways to incrementally hand your mentee, disciple, or follower greater responsibility so you can display increasing trust. Don't throw them in the deep end and expect them to swim.

3. Err on the side of risk, not safety. It is better to give them a little too much trust than hobbling them with too little trust. Throw them in just over their head but next to the shallow end so they don't drown. Be near them when you do it.

4. Make it safe to fail. If trust is based on perpetual success, then trust will never be fully extended. Create a relationship of safety. Communicate honestly but hopefully. Predicate your love on personhood, not performance.

Jesus did not withdraw his trust in Peter even though he knew Peter would deny him three times. Instead, Jesus basically said, "Peter, you are going to blow it, three times. But I have prayed for you. The Spirit will be with you in your failure. I still trust you. And when you have repented, turn back around and strengthen your friends" (Luke 22:32-34).

5. Advocate for their character. One of the most empowering actions leaders can take is to verbally authorize and vouch for their mentee in the presence of others. Risking a bit of your credibility to build their credibility is a powerful act of trust.

Can you imagine how Timothy might have felt as he read Paul's letter of 1 Timothy to the church of Ephesus? "Don't let anyone look down on you because you are young" (1 Timothy 4:12a). Paul is in effect saying, "Timothy, as young as he is, is worthy of all respect, and I trust him."

6. Direct their trust to the Spirit. It is empowering to continually focus your disciple's trust toward the Spirit. You can frequently remind them that a key reason you trust them is because the Spirit of Christ lives in them. If Christ actually lives in them, and if they will rely on his Spirit, then you have ample reason to trust them. Help them trust more deeply in the Spirit.

Jesus used this approach in Mark 13:11 when he said, "Whenever you are arrested and brought to trial, do not worry beforehand about what to say. Just say whatever is given you at the time, for it is not you speaking, but the Holy Spirit." Jesus wasn't trusting them because of their lawyerly skills but because the Spirit was in them.

Our empowering relationships with our mentees, followers, and disciples is built on trust.

Acclaimed author Stephen M.R. Covey writes in his book *The Speed of Trust*: "The first job of a leader—at work or at home—is to inspire trust. It's to bring out the best in people by entrusting them with meaningful stewardships, and to create an environment in which high-trust interaction inspires creativity and possibility."[33]

---

33 https://brandongaille.com/speed-of-trust-summary/ Accessed January 15, 2022.

Jesus unleashed in his followers their "creativity and possibility" as he demonstrated trust in them. We do well to follow his example. It is a key to building our Personal Multiplication Capacity. How can you do this more effectively?

CHAPTER 16

Empowering Training—The Question of Equipping

The prairies of Kansas where I grew up are a long way from the streets of urban Long Beach, where I minister. But an incident in Kansas taught me a valuable ministry lesson that can be applied anywhere.

One hot Kansas afternoon, my friend's pickup accidentally ignited a grass fire that quickly blazed into a small inferno. My friend was able to get a small garden hose to the area, but its trickle of water failed to make any discernible difference. The fire grew until a fire truck arrived and unleashed its massive hose to extinguish the flames.

My friend was willing to fight the fire, but his tools and resources were woefully inadequate for the mission. Likewise, too often we have expected our disciples to quench the fires of hell, but we've handed them a garden hose and said, "Good luck!"

Every follower wants to know, "How will you equip me for the mission?" What tools, training, skills, approaches, and resources can we teach them? How can we resource them to become the men or women God is calling them to be?

Jesus spent three years empowering his disciples to take his mission to the world. He resourced them with the Spirit, words, and skills they would need to effectively take on the hellfire that would confront them.

As we are empowered by the Spirit, we must then consciously channel that empowerment into equipping our disciples or followers with the tools they need. We must stop firing people up unless we also give them the tools to fight the fires. (This has been one of my big mistakes!)

How people learn and grow can be simplified into four stages: hearing, seeing, doing, and teaching. Empowering leaders use all four delivery systems, understanding the effectiveness of each:

1. You learn least from hearing from someone how to do it.

2. You learn more from seeing someone do it.

3. You learn a lot more by doing it yourself.

4. You learn most by teaching someone else how to do it by modeling it for them.

In the empowerment model of Jesus, we see all four forms of training being used.

HEARING: "The Word Alive"

Jesus called his disciples to sit at his feet and hear his teaching. That is what all rabbis did. But Jesus did it differently than the other rabbis. "The crowds were amazed at his teaching, because he taught as one who had authority, and not as their teachers of the law" (Matthew 7:28-29).

Jesus taught the Word as the breath of God, as a spiritual life force. Jesus stated, "The Spirit gives life; the flesh counts for nothing. The words I have spoken to you—they are full of the Spirit and life" (John 6:63). To empower our disciples, we must impart not primarily the *knowledge* of the Word but the *spirit* of the Word.

Have you ever read the Word and felt like it was creating breath in your spiritual lungs? Does your heart beat a little quicker as a phrase catches fire in your soul? If Jesus said that "not even the smallest stroke of the pen" would be accomplished before Heaven and earth disappear (Matthew 5:18), then what kind of spiritual power is ready to jump off the page into our lives? But we must mix the power of the Word with the presence of our faith for this combustion to take place.

Many Christians hear too much of the Word from too many different voices. Their spiritual power is shallow because the raw Word of God is not chewed slowly. We gulp instead of savor. It's a quickly consumed venti instead of a savored demitasse. People become consumers of content rather than meditators on meaning. We hear without listening.

This is the invitation or command Jesus gives to each of the churches in Revelation 2:7: "Whoever has ears, let them hear what the Spirit says to the churches." There is a spiritual listening that leads to spiritual empowerment. To empower others we must teach them to listen deeply to the living Word.

SEEING: "Incarnational Relational" Training

The incarnation was God's Word fully alive in a person. Jesus lived it so they could learn it. Jesus was the truth manifest on Monday mornings, the Spirit demonstrated in the day to day, the wisdom of God in sandals, the supernatural living in the ordinary. The incarnation of God the Son was the pattern for all God's sons and daughters.

But the disciples didn't watch Jesus on the big screen and then seek to do what he did. Empowerment is not mass-produced. The incarnation was relational. Jesus and his disciples ate, hiked, fished, slept, partied, taught, hid out, fed thousands, healed lepers, and adventured ... TOGETHER! We can empower followers to various levels, but to get the power of the 12, we must do a *lot* of life together.

Sean came to Christ under my ministry. He had grown up somewhat on the streets and done some jail time, so Sean and I were as different as can be. Yet, I saw in Sean a unique passion to learn, grow, and serve, so I committed to do my part to empower Sean into the fullness of his calling.

Sean and I have been in small groups, on wild mission trips, in conferences, in 24-hour prayer meetings, in my house eating, playing, laughing, worshiping, fasting, confronting people, comforting people, counseling people, casting out demons, seeing miracles ... the list goes on. Yes, over the last nine years Sean has listened to about a thousand of my sermons, but that's not what has really empowered him. It's been the "incarnational relational," seeing the Word lived (imperfectly, for sure) in my life.

Sean also has had two other significant incarnational relationships that have taught him as much as I have. Sean is now the co-lead pastor of the church that Deb and I led for 31 years. He's doing significant ministry beyond his age in years. Sean, the last person you would pick for leading our church, has become the *ideal* person—because he's been empowered.

DOING: "Seats to Streets" Training

You don't deeply empower disciples through lectures; you empower them through "power encounters." You get them out of their seats and into the streets—out of the classroom and into the scary and sweaty places of real life. These are places where truth turns from theory into activity, where theology becomes biography.

The disciples often heard Jesus teach in the synagogues, but very little is recorded in Scripture about his lessons there. Instead, the disciples write about the practice of the Word on the streets of the towns, the application of the Word in the fields, the encounters where Jesus' teaching upended individuals or entire villages.

I am a sincere fan of classroom learning. My wife and I have doctorates (and loans) to prove it. But I will be the first to say how dangerous the classroom is. If what is taught inside the walls is not practiced in the halls of daily life, it fulfills Paul's warning in 2 Timothy 3:7 about "always learning but never coming to a knowledge of the truth."

It is far too easy to substitute the knowing for the doing, to think that because you have learned it, you have lived it. James 1:23-24 describes it as walking away from the mirror without fixing what the mirror reveals.

Resourcing our disciples happens best in the classroom of action. Teachable moments arise in the rough and tumble reality of life and ministry. The joy and pain of "doing" opens the head and heart for "shaping."

My most impactful theology professor taught physical education. Tim Hansel imparted a biblical view of God that transformed me: God was to be experienced daily in small and large ways, in the ordinary encounters of life. Tim would proceed to tell us of his latest adventures of serving God outside the classroom. Then he would share what God had taught him. Then *we* had to go out and "adventure with God." We had to reflect on it, write about it, and share it with the class. Tim often said, "Daring to do is deciding to learn."

Jesus empowered his disciples by sending them out to do the real stuff of ministry. He sent them out when they were still novices. He gave them authority, but it was unseasoned authority. He knew that they couldn't grow unless they were stretched—asked to do what was beyond them. The real learning was in the real doing. Sometimes they had victories, and sometimes they had failures (Luke 9:40), but they were learning forward.

In Luke 10:19, Jesus looks at the 72 disciples and says, "I have given you authority to trample on snakes and scorpions and to overcome all the power of the enemy; nothing will harm you." They took that authority and did some powerful spiritual ministry.

Teaching our disciples to lean into their spiritual authority is vital to their empowerment. This authority is from Jesus himself. They will not learn the power of this authority in their seats, but in the streets. That authority is not predicated on how experienced or knowledgable they are. They must exercise it to grow in it.

TEACHING: "Training Trainers"

There is a vast difference between teaching disciples to learn and training disciples to disciple. Jesus taught his disciples truth, but more important, he trained his disciples to do with others what he had done with them. You don't start a world movement by creating 12 *Jeopardy* winners who know a lot. You launch a multiplying movement by training ordinary people to train ordinary people.

Our training models are usually focused on addition instead of multiplication. We add to our knowledge, our character, our spiritual giftedness. But multiplication demands that we grow as trainers. I concur with the Navigators, a disciple-making ministry, in saying that you haven't made a disciple until your disciple makes a disciple.

As a high schooler I was taught how to share a well-known evangelist tract, "The Four Spiritual Laws." I learned it and tried it a few times before basically stuffing it in the back of my dresser drawer. But then I was invited to go to Dallas with all expenses paid to attend a huge conference: Expo 72, which was a defining gathering in the Jesus

People Movement. The catch was that I had to share the Four Spiritual Laws with people in Dallas neighborhoods, *and* I had to take other local high school students with me to train them how to do it.

Suddenly I was a sponge. I wanted to learn all I could as deeply as I could. Why? Because I was going to be sharing it and teaching other high schoolers how to teach it. When the week in Dallas arrived, our little team hit the streets going door to door to share Jesus with people. God was faithful, and we saw people pray to receive Christ. But the *real* measure of my effectiveness was in those students I had trained taking it back home to train others.

You learn differently when you intend to train others with what you are learning. So resourcing our followers must include training them how to train others.

Empowering leaders prioritize supernatural provision *and* natural preparation. This is the blend we see in Paul's empowering leadership of Timothy. On one hand, Paul essentially said, "Timothy, Don't neglect that gift that was given to you supernaturally by the Spirit when we laid our hands on you!" (1 Timothy 4:14). But then in the next verse Paul says, "Be diligent in these matters; give yourself wholly to them, so that everyone may see your progress" (v. 15).

Paul was big on the supernatural provision and on the training process. He had one of the highest Personal Multiplication Capacities of anyone since Jesus—in part because he was focused on multiplication more than addition. He directed Timothy to take his gift and use it to multiply more than add.

We see this most clearly in the oft-cited 2 Timothy 2:2: "And the things you have heard me say in the presence of many witnesses entrust to reliable people who will also be qualified to teach others." Paul is saying, "Timothy, the goal is not to teach as many people as you can (addition). It is to train as many teachers as you can (multiplication)."

Paul trained Timothy to be a trainer of trainers, not just a teacher. Paul's method of resourcing was this dynamic combination of historic instruction (Old Testament truths brought into New Testament realities) and incarnational experience (personal, lived-out realities of his ongoing encounter with the Spirit of Jesus).

5 EMPOWERING PRACTICES TO SUPPORT RESOURCING

1. Develop day-to-day discipleship. When possible, involve disciples in your day-to-day life and include spiritual discussions along the way.

2. Share ministry moments. Take disciples with you into ministry moments and spiritual adventures, then debrief to see what was learned.

3. Remember that readers are leaders. Develop a highly selective reading list of books on subjects you want disciples to learn about. Read and debrief the learnings together.

4. Practice cross-mentoring. Enlist the help of other leaders with expertise in areas in which you want your disciples to grow. It takes a team to fully and healthily mentor and develop a disciple.

5. Create learning opportunities. Take or send your disciples to conferences, workshops, seminary classes, etc. for learning and skill-building in areas in which they need to be equipped.

If you fail to train your disciples/mentees/followers toward the expectation and goal of multiplying, you will be creating consumers who may add to the Kingdom but who will never start the generational multiplication that Jesus calls them to. How well are you resourcing those who look to you to lead them?

CHAPTER 17

Empowering Opportunities— The Question of Open Doors

Mark was a highly successful milk salesman who could talk to anyone. As he started coming to our church, I began a mentoring relationship with Mark. I encouraged him to become a small group leader. Shortly thereafter, I opened a role for him as a small group coach. He excelled at both. I started giving him opportunities for teaching and preaching.

Several months later, after many hours together as friends and co-laborers, I asked Mark to consider becoming the part-time associate pastor in our new Sunday evening church plant. He accepted and even eventually left his lucrative sales position to join us full time. Within three years, I turned the lead pastor role over to Mark.

Mark knew I loved him. We were on mission together, and he trusted me. I was resourcing him. But for Mark to be more fully empowered, I had to open doors for him. Without these open doors of opportunity, Mark would probably have plateaued in his ministry impact.

Every follower wants to know, "Are there doors of opportunity you can open for me?" Jesus was the master door opener. Throughout his time with his disciples, he was continually offering them opportunities they would never have had without him. He opened doors by sending them out with his power to reach villages with the good news (Luke 10), having them give directions to a hungry crowd of 5,000 before a miraculous feast (Matthew 14), challenging them to cast out demons (Mark 6:13), inviting them to walk on water (Matthew 14), joining him in prayer in a world-changing moment (Mark 14), and showing them how to stand before the most powerful leaders in the nation (Mark 11). They were empowered as they operated in the midst of increasingly more significant and challenging situations. Empowering leaders are always looking for doors they can open for others.

Early in my ministry a prophecy was given over me that said I was in a small room, but God was moving me to larger and larger rooms. It also said that I would have to move through doors that only one of his servants could open for me. I could not open them, but I could trust God to send a door opener. Indeed this is what happened. I began to look for doors that God wanted me to go through and for empowering leaders who would open them for me.

I am keenly aware that any increase in my ministry influence has been due to the empowering leaders in my life—leaders who dared to take a risk and use their influence, authority, or networks to open doors so that I could use the gifts God had given me.

Barnabas was a significant "door opener" in the early church. Remember how Paul tried to join the disciples in Jerusalem, but (out of fear) their doors were locked to him? Enter Barnabas the empowering leader. He found Paul, brought him to the disciples, knocked at their door, and essentially said, "I want you to meet my friend, Paul" (Acts 9). Barnabas opened the door for Paul to minister in Antioch (Acts 11). It was Barnabas who opened (or reopened) the door of missionary work for John Mark (Acts 15).

Not long after Deb and I received the "river" vision (described in Chapter 11), I had another vivid vision. I was standing on a grassy hill looking at the far horizon. I suddenly turned around, and behind me I saw a high wall that stretched for 100 yards. The wall was filled with doors. These doors were of all different sizes, shapes, and colors—there were purple squares, big red circles, small orange triangles, skinny yellow rectangles, etc. I stared and wondered about what I was seeing.

When I turned to look at the horizon again, I saw a mass of people coming my direction. The closer they came, the more I began to see that these people were different sizes, shapes, and colors. Some were purple squares, big red circles, small orange triangles, skinny yellow rectangles, etc. I then saw myself begin to direct the individuals to the door that fit them. When I opened the door for them, they were gone. I recognized my call was to simply be a doorkeeper, a door opener, so people could flow through and go to bring life somewhere else—because as Ezekiel 47:9 declares, "Where the river flows everything will live."

Since then I have sought to find people's shape and calling, then to open doors for them, even if those doors take them to other ministries, churches, and denominations. All types of ministry have been birthed through uniquely gifted people who just needed an open door. But the surprising fact is that the more doors we opened for others, the more our church was multiplied.

Anyone can be a door-opener for others, and it's one of the most empowering moves you can make. The empowerment of the Spirit can cause your eyes to see doors for others that you never would have seen if you weren't seeking to be an empowering leader.

5 EMPOWERING PRACTICES TO PROVIDE OPPORTUNITIES

1. Look for outside doors. There is value in opening doors for volunteer positions within church ministries and programs. But the *real* empowerment happens when you open doors of opportunity outside the safety zone of the church, when you send disciples to the "villages" (Luke 10).

2. Pray for open doors. Ask the Lord to reveal doors and to open doors for the gospel message and for disciple-making. Paul requested this in Colossians 4:3—"And pray for us, too, that God may open a door for our message, so that we may proclaim the mystery of Christ, for which I am in chains."

3. Share the door. Often an open door, an opportunity, comes to us that wouldn't come to one of our mentees. While we can't send them through our open door, we can share it with them. I have often asked a mentee to share a preaching slot, a ministry assignment, a witnessing project, or a mission trip leadership role with me.

4. Build doors. A helpful way to open doors is by creating ministry projects where leadership is demanded. I have used my credibility and resources to cast a vision for a local or global mission project and then assigned one of my mentees to lead it.

5. Knock on doors. Ask ministry partners, parachurch ministries, community partners, other churches if they have a role of leadership where your disciple might be a good fit.

The idea is to empower your disciple/mentee/student into bigger rooms of influence by seeing them walk through more open doors. Ask yourself whether you truly want them to walk through doors that lead them into rooms bigger than the one you are ministering in. This was Jesus' desire. "Very truly I tell you, whoever believes in me will do the works I have been doing, and they will do even greater things than these, because I am going to the Father" (John 14:12).

Wanting your disciple to do greater things than you is the mark of a truly empowering leader. Is that your desire?

CHAPTER 18

Empowering Relationships—The Question of Team

One of my favorite chapters in the New Testament may seem to be a strange choice, but it is Romans 16. Here the apostle Paul opens a window into his heart and into his ministry strategy. He lists 29 leaders by name, expressing his love for them, honoring their contributions to building the church and underlining that they were teammates on this mission.

Romans 16 is a chapter where Paul reveals that he had a high priority on empowering others and a key way he did so was to connect his disciples with other teammates. There was no thought of possessiveness on Paul's part. Our followers, mentees, and disciples need more than a single leader.

Every follower wants to know, "Who can you connect me with to empower me into the fullness of God's potential for me?" Barnabas was one of the most empowering leaders in the New Testament. He was frequently introducing someone to someone else so that the mission could advance. He was a master networker on behalf of others. He didn't just open doors; he opened hearts.

Barnabas gave what he had but introduced others who could give what they had. There was no leadership territoriality in Barnabas. One passage that is often overlooked is Acts 11:22-25. Barnabas travels from Jerusalem to Antioch to see these new Grecian believers. Of course, once he gets there he encourages them. It appears that he becomes the new de facto leader of Antioch because verse 24 tells us, "He was a good man, full of the Holy Spirit and faith, and a great number of people were brought to the Lord."

Most pastors today would have stopped right there—new church, my people, great numbers. But not Barnabas. Acts 11:25-26a tells us, "Then Barnabas went to Tarsus to look for Saul, and when he found him, he brought him to Antioch. So for a whole year Barnabas and Saul met with the church and taught great numbers of people." Barnabas shared leadership with Saul for a year, and Saul undoubtedly furthered his theology and his skills in that year-long practicum.

But then Barnabas adds to the team again. He and Saul (in Acts 12:25) return to Antioch from a Jerusalem trip, taking John Mark with them. Now Saul has a mentor in Barnabas and a mentee in John Mark. But when they get back to Antioch, we discover that Saul also has some ministry peers in Simeon, Niger, Lucius, and Manaen. What a gospel team—all brought together by Barnabas, an empowered leader who was also empowering.

To be fully empowered, our disciples need this same three-directional team (3D leadership): spiritual friends walking AHEAD of them, BESIDE them, and BEHIND them. A 3D team of mentors, mentees, and ministry peers all together on the same mission.

Eric Marsh was the best-known Christian leader in Long Beach when he introduced me to Todd Wilson, the former CEO of Exponential (who became a mentor to me). Todd introduced me to Bill Couchenour, one of the most networked leaders in American Christianity. Bill became a ministry peer, but he also introduced me to the legendary church multiplier Ralph Moore, who has poured wisdom into me. For the past seven years, we've all been a Kingdom team. We have had the joy of taking nearly 1,000 church leaders through a learning community experience focused on Kingdom multiplication. My life and the Church of Jesus have benefited from our efforts. I have felt empowered to a whole new level. I have now introduced my disciples and pastoral successors, Joel Silva and Sean Fenner, to all these men. This is the way empowering leadership works.

When leaders choose to create Kingdom connections for their followers, great things happen! As we seek to be empowered and to be empowering, it's helpful to keep this 3D leadership concept at the front of our thinking. When leaders prioritize the three dimensions of relationships—*ahead, beside, behind*—they surround their followers with the team they need to thrive and produce much Kingdom fruit.

One of the greatest studies in leadership is Moses. He was an empowered leader who empowered others. Study his leadership constellation, and you'll find his mother and Jethro as mentors to him, Aaron and Hur as ministry peers who stood beside him, and Joshua and Caleb as mentees who he passed off leadership and influence to. When we lead with these three-dimensional relationships in mind, we receive and transfer maximum power.

After nearly 31 years of pastoring, Deb and I passed on the leadership of our church to two dynamic leaders in their early 30s. Our confidence to do so was based on the health we saw in them in all three of these dimensions of relationships. These leaders were not alone. They were learning from excellent mentors, beyond us. They enjoyed healthy friendships with ministry peers. They had demonstrated empowering investment into multiple disciples and mentees. They were ready!

5 EMPOWERING PRACTICES TO ENCOURAGE 3D TEAMS

1. Stress the limitations of solo leadership. Our culture celebrates individualism and solo celebrities. This makes it the default desire of most aspiring disciples and leaders. We must counteract that non-biblical and destructive undertow. Using the New Testament pattern of Jesus, the early church, and the apostolic mission, we teach the power, purity, and beauty of leading in a team constellation.

2. Teach the essentiality of 3D teammaking. Helping our followers to think in terms of mentors, peers, and mentees encourages them to be building a team around them that will help them grow, sustain, and influence.

3. Keep your connection radar on. When you meet new people, keep your disciples in mind. Is this someone who can teach them, support them, partner with them, or follow them? What can this person contribute to those God has entrusted me to mentor?

4. Pray with your mentee for the development of their team. When you actively pray with your disciple about who they partner with, it accomplishes three objectives. First, it asks the Lord for his assistance in team-building. Second, it demonstrates your belief that they need more than you for their empowerment. It works against your pride and their codependency. Third, it raises their awareness to be looking for those they can link arms with.

5. Ask the unasked question that unlocks an otherwise missed relationship. There is a question that empowering leaders ask regularly: "Who do you know that I need to know?" This question catapults you into unknown networks of relationships that often hold substantial value for you or your mentee.

CHAPTER 19

The Empowering Pay-off— The Question of Reward

When I was training for my first marathon I was asked by several people, "Is it worth it?" In other words, what will my payoff be for hours and hours and miles and miles of pounding the pavement in my Nikes? After all, I won't be fast enough to place in even the top 100; I won't win any money for finishing; I won't get my name in the paper (this was before I could even broadcast it on Instagram or Facebook); and I will be so sore I can hardly walk for a few days after. Is it worth it?

It was a question of reward, of pay-off. What was the reward for the sacrifice? It is a human question. It is a legitimate question. It is a question that pleases God. It is a question that Jesus and the apostles addressed frequently and appealed to fervently. God wired us to care about ROI, return on investment.

Every follower wants to know, "Will it be worth it in the end?"
When Peter asks Jesus, "We have left everything to follow you! What then will there be for us?" (Matthew 19:27), Jesus doesn't rebuke him.

He motivates him by speaking of the thrones they will sit on and of gaining 100 times as much of whatever they have sacrificed.

Of course, as Paul boldly proclaims, humans are all in a race, a life-long marathon. This race can be run in such a way that we receive an eternal reward. "Do you not know that in a race all the runners run, but only one gets the prize? Run in such a way as to get the prize. Everyone who competes in the games goes into strict training. They do it to get a crown that will not last, but we do it to get a crown that will last forever" (1 Corinthians 9:24-25).

Those who won in the Olympics of Paul's time were given a victor's wreath made of olive branches. It was a great honor to win, but within a few days the olive branch crown withered, dried up, and began to fall apart. This is the contrast Paul is underlining. When we seek to increase our PMC, to live more empowered and to empower others more, we are running for a glorious, eternal crown.

This truth should be highly motivating to us personally, but it also must be a key in our equipping. We must continually exhort our disciples to have a heavenly mindset, to set their hearts and their minds "on things above" (Colossians 3:1-2).

You have probably heard it said, "They are so heavenly minded they are of no earthly good." It's a lie. Believers who truly understand, prioritize, and contemplate Heaven will be of the most earthly good. The lives of all the heroes of Hebrews 11 shout this truth. Take Moses as one example. "He regarded disgrace for the sake of Christ as of greater value than the treasures of Egypt, because he was looking ahead to his reward" (Hebrews 11:26).

Unfortunately, with the rise of the internet, the accessibility to notoriety has increased dramatically. The possibility of becoming "known," "liked," and "followed" has tickled the ego of Christian leaders. It has drawn them away from the deep waters of "life-on-life discipleship" to the shallowness of being a "social media influencer." They have Diotrephes disease. John described Diotrephes as one "who loves to be first." Too many leaders today want to be first and, consequently, have an insipid, short-term addition mindset instead of a generational, multiplicative mindset. They are chasing the olive-branch crown instead of the eternal one.

Cheap, easy, fast, and selfish or costly, difficult, slow, and selfless? This is the grave choice that Paul sets before us: "For no one can lay any foundation other than the one already laid, which is Jesus Christ. If anyone builds on this foundation using gold, silver, costly stones, wood, hay or straw, their work will be shown for what it is, because the Day will bring it to light. It will be revealed with fire, and the fire will test the quality of each person's work. If what has been built survives, the builder will receive a reward" (1 Corinthians 3:11-14).

Christ is the only foundation, but some want to build a name for themselves on the foundation of Christ. Paul is saying that is like flammable straw. Whatever you have built for self will burn. But those who seek to build the lives of others on the foundation of Christ—now that's inflammable gold.

It's not the quantity of your ministry but the *quality* of your ministry that is leading toward reward. Quality is empowering others to multiply their life of faith in others. That is often sacrificial, slow, and selfless, but once that flywheel starts turning, it creates rapid Kingdom expansion.

As much as our mindset must be focused above, Jesus did not limit his promises of rewards to the happy hereafter of Heaven. There are rewards here and now that need to be taught and modeled to those we are empowering. Read these two verses slowly: "'Truly I tell you,' Jesus replied, 'No one who has left home or brothers or sisters or mother or father or children or fields for me and the gospel will fail to receive a hundred times as much in this present age: homes, brothers, sisters, mothers, children and fields—along with persecutions—and in the age to come eternal life'" (Mark 10:29-30).

None of the disciples ended up with 100 houses to rent out or 100 vacation homes. Neither will we. But by sacrificing for Christ, his church, and his mission, we will enjoy great rewards here and now—rewards such as the joy of a global family, of friends who love you before you meet them, of thousands of homes that would joyfully host you. These all become yours. This is not just a theory. Having traveled across the world, I know this to be true, and I count myself a rich man because of it.

Living in the smile of God is certainly the richest present blessing. To sense yourself following in Jesus' steps and giving your life to do what he did during his life brings deep satisfaction. Having a centeredness; a healthy identity that is not based on your performance; an indescribable love, joy, and peace; a cause worth trading your life for that blesses you and others now and forever—the list of rewards goes on!

John the apostle tells us his greatest joy in life and thereby gives us insight into one of the greatest rewards of living with a high PMC. John declares, "I have no greater joy than to hear that my children are walking in the truth" (3 John 1:4). To have spiritual children who are living their lives for God's truth and who are reproducing that life in others is a reward that makes our hearts sing. It makes all the investments, prayers, and time worth it.

5 EMPOWERING PRACTICES TO FOCUS ON REWARD

1. Frequently revisit the WHY of disciple-making and missional living. Emphasize the joy of obedience because of the Lord's worthiness, regardless of the payoff in life. Our salvation is a reward worthy of all our service, even if no other rewards were ever to be experienced.

2. Frequently ask, "Where is life better, and where are you experiencing joy because you are following your call?" Help your disciple become a "good-finder" and "gratitude collector."

3. Share your own stories of reward. Talk about things that have come from investing your life in others for the sake of advancing the Kingdom. Ask others to share stories from small spiritual encounters that brought them a blessing.

4. Pray consistently with your disciple/mentee. Ask for eyes to see the goodness of God in the present and glories of God in the eternal. Pray through Scriptures that deal with rewards and Heaven.

5. Memorize Scripture with your disciple. Choose two or three verses that underline the rewards to come now and later to those who are faithful.

Back to my marathon training ... When people inquired, "Is it worth it? Why are you doing it?" My answer was a quote from an Oscar-winning movie that had come out just a few years before: *Chariots of Fire*, the true story of Scottish Christian missionary and Olympic gold medalist, Eric Liddell. In the movie, Liddell explains his motive for running: "When I run, I feel God's pleasure."

As followers of Christ, we have entered the race Hebrews 12:1-2 describes. The only way to run it is by "fixing our eyes on Jesus." Jesus ran his race with a focus on the reward, "the joy set before him." His joy was pleasing his Father and bringing those he loved to Heaven. A similar reward is available to us. How well do you point others toward it?

CHAPTER 20

The Final Product—Your Highest Kingdom Impact

As a fellow Christ follower, I know what you truly desire. I could describe it using a title from one of the most popular Christian books ever written, *My Utmost for His Highest* by Oswald Chambers. Chambers only lived to age 43, yet 100 years later his words continue to empower believers to give their "utmost for his highest." We want that, don't we? We want to use our brief lives for God's highest glory.

The book before you has been written to help us produce the largest "product" possible with our lives. Remember that a "product" is the mathematical term for the result when you multiply two numbers together. I have suggested a way of thinking and living that multiplies your vertical y number by your horizontal x number to produce a "product" called Personal Multiplication Capacity.

Living each day as EMPOWERED by the Spirit as possible (your y number) multiplied by seeking each day to be as EMPOWERING as possible to those in your circles of influence (your x number) will create the highest PMC possible. This in turn will give you a life of the greatest Kingdom impact.

This tool is not really about *y* or *x* or PMC numbers; it's about instilling a personal paradigm, a mindset that will direct our daily lives. It is living in the intersection of two prayers: "Fill me, Spirit" and "Use me, Spirit, to empower others." The "product" is the multiplication of the Kingdom.

In my personal ministry story, I left you at the point of transitioning from a "lake" church to a "river" church, focused on multiplying disciples, leaders, and churches. That transition was not easy, but the Lord helped us, and since 1999 our church has been flowing. We are roughly the same attendance size we were back in 1999, *but* the Kingdom has advanced exponentially!

With a commitment to be an empowered church and to be empowering to all the saints God gives us, we have planted one or two churches every year since 1999. Now some of them are having babies, and our international church planting has averaged three or four churches every year. Also, we have sent over 70 pastors, ministers, and missionaries into full-time service.

My dream of leading a megachurch was far too small. By pursuing multiplication, we have thousands of believers in our generational lineage, and our church still only has 39 parking spaces. Two of my sons in the faith are taking the church further than I ever did.

Your ministry role may be very different from mine, but the principles are the same. Your "utmost for his highest" means receiving the promise and calling of Acts 1:8 every day. Be empowered to go empower others.

May the Spirit fill and use you beyond what you could dream or imagine!

Additional Resources
EXPONENTIAL BOOKS BY LARRY WALKEMEYER

Flow: Unleashing a River of Multiplication in Your Church, Your City and World

The Mobilization Flywheel: Creating a Culture of Mobilization

Beyond 4: Leading Your Church to Level 5 Multiplication

Play Thuno: The World-Changing Multiplication Game

Together with God: Living in the Power of Jesus' Greatest Prayer

Together with Family: Flourishing in a Level Five Marriage

21 Days Of Empowerment: A Guide for Moving with the Spirit

Made for More Visual Guide

Led: Going With the Spirit (Engaging the Power of the Spirit in Evangelism)

About the Author

Dr. Larry Walkemeyer serves as the Strategic Catalyst for Multiplication for Free Methodist USA encouraging the multiplication of disciples, leaders and churches nationally and is on the Executive Leadership Team of the Free Methodist USA.

He is also Global Pastor for Light & Life Church, Long Beach, CA., a multiplying, multi-ethnic, urban church he and his wife Deb led for the past 30 years. During their tenure the church grew dynamically, and planted churches both nationally and globally.

As Director of Equipping and Spiritual Engagement for Exponential (the world's largest church planting resource group), Larry seeks to influence the church of Jesus toward multiplication. Holding a doctorate in church leadership and as the author/co-author of ten books, Larry speaks and consults frequently across the USA.

Azusa Pacific University, from which Larry holds a Doctorate of Ministry, has recognized Larry with the Centennial Award, naming him one of the most influential graduates in its history. Larry serves on the Executive Committee of the Board of Trustees for Azusa Pacific University.

Larry and Dr. Deb Walkemeyer have been married since 1978. They write and speak frequently on marriage, ministry, and leadership. They have two amazing adult daughters. Larry enjoys biking, working out, snow skiing, waterskiing, boating, and traveling.

Made in the USA
Monee, IL
05 March 2024

54477544R00095